IVORY COAST

Regina Fuchs

BRADT PUBLICATIONS, UK
HUNTER PUBLISHING, USA

First published in English in 1991 by Bradt Publications, 41 Nortoft Rd, Chalfont St. Peter, Bucks, SL9 OLA, England from the German original by Conrad Stein Verlag, Kiel.
Distributed in the USA by Hunter Publishing Inc.

Copyright © 1991 Conrad Stein Verlag

All rights reserved. No part of this publication may be reproduced, stored in a retrieval system, or transmitted in any form or by any means, electronic, mechanical, photocopying or otherwise without the written permission of the publisher.

ISBN 0-946983-53-4

Translated from the German by Erika Miers
Photographs by the author
Maps by Gunda Siebke

ABOUT THE AUTHOR

Regina Fuchs, born in 1958, works as a travel agent and has travelled in Africa for several years. She recently spent many months in Ivory Coast, relying on public transport to travel around the country and experience at first hand another part of the fascinating continent.

PREFACE

The Ivory Coast is one of the most exotic and culturally interesting countries in Africa. Wonderful palm beaches, one of the last virgin rain forests of West Africa, broad savannas, mountain areas with mysterious myths surrounding dances, masks and liana bridges; impressive craftsmanship and music all characterize this land.

Progress and deeply rooted traditions join hands here. First and foremost is the encounter with the lovely people and the multitude of impressions of African daily life.

Not everything is perfect in this country but who would want that? If you are looking for a safari adventure or developed coastal resorts, as in East Africa, then you will be disappointed. There are few things to visit, but there is plenty to look at and experience.

The country has opened itself up very slowly to tourism and rough, dusty tracks still lead to its most beautiful and largely unspoiled beaches on the Gulf of Guinea.

This book will give you some useful facts about the Ivory Coast. Africa is a pulsating, lively continent full of contrasting riddles, secrets and new experiences.

Travelling in Africa means improvising, every day and every time in a new way. If you are open to information about the region and about their culture, then you will learn and understand. Spontaneity and patience is a must. An African proverb says: "There is nothing more than time, because there is always more time."

This travel guide is full of 'up to date' information which will soon be 'out of date'. But I trust they will remain comparative. All the views expressed are subjective and based on my own personal experiences, since each sees a foreign country in a different way. I would, therefore, be grateful for any tips, additions or suggestions for improvement.

I would like to thank my friends from the Ivory Coast who supported me in gathering information and helped me come closer to this country.

I hope you will enjoy the Ivory Coast as much as I did.

Akwaba! - Welcome - and the people of the Ivory Coast mean it!

Regina Fuchs

Contents

Part 1: The Country — 7
Geography — 7
History — 7
The People — 10
Religion — 11
Political Structure — 14
Language — 15
Economy — 15
Business Hours — 16
The Flora and Fauna — 17
Planning and preparation — **21**
Entry Requirements/Customs — 21
Arrival — 21
Important Addresses — 22
Money/Currency — 23
Climate and Time for Travelling — 24
Average Temperatures — 25
Health — 25
Vaccinations — 25
General Health Tips — 27
Checklist for First Aid — 30
Luggage — 30
Documents — 31
Equipment Checklist, Clothing — 31
Checklist — 32
In Ivory Coast — **35**
Travel within the Country — 35
Food and Beverages — 38
Shopping and Bargaining — 40
Mail and Telephone — 41
Photography — 44
Accommodation — 45

Part 2: Regional Guide — **47**
Abidjan — 47
Plateau, Treichville — 48
Adjamé — 52

Contents

Near Abidjan	59
The Banco National Park, Plage de Vridi	59
East of Abidjan	59
Grand Bassam	59
Assinie	63
Bingerville, Bregbo	64
Aboisso	65
The Western Coastal Region	65
Jacqueville	65
Ile de Tiegba	66
Grand Lahou	67
Sassandra	68
San Pedro	70
Grand Béréby	71
Tabou, Boubélé	72
The Central Region	73
Yamoussoukro	73
Bouaké	74
Katiola	75
Bouaflé, Daloa	76
The Western Region	76
Man	80
Area Around Man	81
Danané, Tai National Park	82
Biankouma, Gouessesso, Touba	83
The Northern Region	84
Odiénné	86
Area Around Odiénné, Boundiali	87
Korhogo	88
Area Around Korhogo	92
Waraniéné, Koni	92
Kasombarga, Torgokaha, Fakaha	92
Niofouin, Tortiya, Ferkéssédougou	93
Kong, Comoé National Park	94
The Eastern Region	98
Abengourou	98
Bondoukou	100
Bouna	102
Appendix	**103**
Index	**105**

VI

PART 1

The Country

GEOGRAPHY

The Ivory Coast, (**Côte d'Ivoire** is the official name) lies on the Gulf of Guinea and covers an area of 322,463 km^2. It lies between 5° and 11° latitude north and 3° and 8° longitude west and is square-shaped.

The longest north-south distance is about 700 km, the broadest east-west distance approximately 650 km. Côte d'Ivoire is bordered by Ghana in the east, Burkina Faso and Mali in the north, and Guinea and Liberia in the west. The official administrative capital has been **Yamoussoukro** since 1983.

HISTORY

Before colonization by France, the northern uninhabited savanna-like region of the Ivory Coast was part of the Mali kingdom. In the large jungle area in the south and west there were no settlements.

Oral tradition tells of a small native people, who now rule the forests as ghosts. Their descendants, the **Gagou**, along with the Dan in the west belong to the earliest settlers in the country. Around the 11th century the Senoufo from the banks of the Niger River settled in the north, in order to escape from Islamic influences.

In around 1600 these peaceful farming people were forced into a dispute over their land by the Malinké, a warring people from the Sahel zone. The Malinké gained control over the trade routes of the south for coconuts, weapons and gold and those of the north for slaves, cattle and transport animals. In so doing the Malinké (also known as Dioula) created an impressive kingdom and settled throughout the country. Shortly thereafter they converted to Islam and founded important Islamic centres with the city of Kong as their capital.

The Country

In time other areas were settled. First the Lobi, a hunting and nomadic tribe, made their way into the northeast area of Bouna in the 16th century. Then, after inheritance disputes, the descendants of the Ashanti tribe came from the Gold Coast, (today's Ghana), and settled between Aboisso and Abengourou. Here they were found in the 18th century by the Baoule, another tribe from Ghana who tried to make their way further west. According to legend they were blocked in their journey along the Couoé River, so Queen Polou had to sacrifice her child to the gods in order to continue their journey. Her cry "Baoule" ("the child is dead") became the name of the people.

From the east came today's lagoon tribes who met up with the widely-branched Kru tribe in the west, who came from what is today Liberia. These coastal people were the first to be met by Europeans exploring the Gulf of Guinea.

The Portuguese, Dutch and English arrived and quickly turned their back on the seemingly impenetrable "coast of evil men", as it was called. It is true that in Jacqueville, Grand Lahou and Sassandra a few outposts for the slave trade were established, but for the most part this tragic episode of history took place further east along the Gold Coast.

Already by the 17th century the first French missionaries had landed on the Ivory Coast, but it was not until 1830 that the French began to explore the hinterland. The first **trading post** was established in **Grand Bassam** in 1842. By the end of the 19th century France had signed an alliance pact with almost all of the tribal leaders. The envoy Treich-Lapléne and Chief Binger, the first governor of the country, experienced very belligerent resistance from the influential ritual leader Samory Touré, who had already taken over a large part of the country. He was captured and arrested and in 1893 the country was given the name Côte d'Ivoire and declared a **French colony**.

In 1898 a yellow fever epidemic swept through Grand Bassam and Bingerville was chosen as the new capital. It was only after the construction of the railways that Abidjan became the capital of the colony in 1934.

In 1958 the Ivory Coast became an autonomous republic and achieved complete **independence** on August 7, 1960 under the

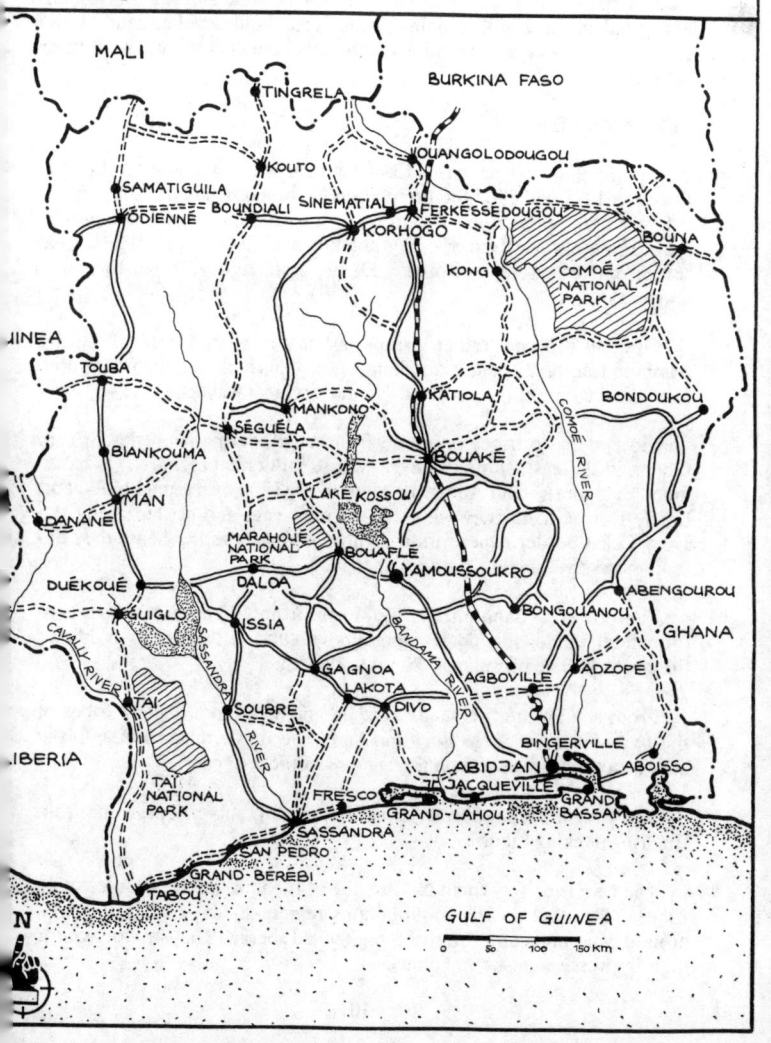

leadership of Felix Houphouet-Boigny, who became and still is president and head of state. The political and economic development of the country maintains a close and continuous connection with its former colonial power, France.

THE PEOPLE

The population of the Ivory Coast is estimated at about 11 million. Between 1975 and 1985 the population increased by about 50%, the result of an economic boom and an increase in immigrants. Approximately one third of the population lives in the cities. The largest settlements are Abidjan, Bouaké, Daloa, Man, Agboville, Korhogo and Gagnoa.

Over **60 different tribal groups** live in the Ivory Coast, all having common traditions, beliefs and languages. There has been considerable intermarriage recently, particularly amongst city dwellers.

Most of these tribes originate from neighbouring countries. From Ghana in the east, came the **Agni**, whose influential monarchy is based near Abengourou and Aboisso. After the division of the mighty Ashanti family from Ghana they were forced into exile and settled along the Ivory Coast border, where today, with a monarch as the head, they defend themselves against modern change.

The powerful **Baoulé** tribe, also came from Ghana in the 18th century under the leadership of queen Poukou and settled in the middle of the country. The president belongs to this tribe.

From southeastern Ghana came the many different lagoon tribes of the Ivory Coast, of these **Ebri** and **Fanti** live mostly from fishing in the area around Abidjan and on the lagoons of the east coast.

The **Kru** in the southwest, divided into many sub-groups, came from English-speaking Liberia.

The **Dan** tribe (or Yacouba) are one of the most culturally interesting tribes. They live in the mountainous region of the west in the area around Man and came from the region of Liberia. They are known for their impressive masks and dances.

The Country

The northeast and northwest of the Ivory Coast is the home of the large **Malinké** group, also called **Dioula** (in reference to their trade). These tribes came between the 16th and 18th centuries via the trade routes along the Niger River from the Sahel region, attracted by the wealth of gold and cola nuts in the Ivory Coast. Soon after their arrival they converted to the **Moslem faith** and created many important Islamic centres.

In the far northeast the **Lobi**, nomads and hunters, have preserved many of their traditions and unique clay architecture.

The **Senoufo** living around Korhogo are well known as followers of animism and their ritual beliefs are expressed in the Poro cult (see *Religion*). They are farmers and remarkable artists. Throughout the centuries they have kept their own culture still in the form of traditional architecture, dance and music, art and language.

The average population density is around 30 to 40 inhabitants/km^2, the least settled area is in the northeastern part of the country with fewer than 5 inhabitants/km^2. Abidjan, which is almost bursting at the seams has more than 350 inhabitants/km^2. The continuing influx of Africans from neighbouring countries attracted by economic growth, has become a problem for the city in the last few decades. Overpopulated slums are a direct contrast to the well developed and new administrative and business centres.

Today, approx. 2 million foreign Africans live here as well as a large number of Lebanese businessmen who came at the turn of the century to French West Africa.

Despite the large social differences amongst the population, the Ivory Coast has been able to keep a comparatively high rate of economic and political stability.

RELIGION

Approximately 65% of the population of the Ivory Coast follow traditional African religions. Believers think that events in one's life have a supernatural cause. Even inanimate objects possess a soul and spirit and have a positive and negative effect on the living.

In these religions **ancestor worship** plays a very important role. The dead continue to exist as spiritual powers and are in constant contact with the living. Through sacrificial rituals and dances worshippers pray for the protection of the spirits and ask for blessings. The traditional beliefs have a substantial influence on the social system within the tribes. This is expressed especially in the *Poro* cult of the Senoufo tribes.

Poro means the process of maturing into adulthood. It is a system of up-bringing divided into three time periods, each seven years long and ending with initiation (ceremony of maturity). Since in the eyes of the Senoufo a person is considered an animal from birth, the children are raised out of this stage and prepared for life in the community through *Poro*. The most important goals are self-control, taking over duties in social life and philosophical reflection.

The rituals and tests of *Poro* are exercised in a **"Holy Forest"**, which can be found near each village. Dances using masks and secret alliances play a large rôle and those uninitiated are not allowed to attend.

Since the 18th century **Islam** has spread quite extensively among the Malinké tribes in the north of the Ivory Coast. Moslems are distributed throughout the country and represent about 23% of the population. Like the traditional religions Islam also allows for polygamy.

Only about 12% of the people of the Ivory Coast confess to **Christianity**. Among them there is a small minority who are members of sects derived from the Christian faith (e.g. Harrism).

Since a dominant traditional consciousness prevails throughout the country, the different religions are not completely separate, ideas frequently overlap. I often came upon people who described themselves as Christians but who had several wives.

POLITICAL STRUCTURE

The political system of the Ivory Coast is characterized as a **presidential regime**. The president of the republic determines all governmental policies, is commander-in-chief of the military, practises executive powers and is chairman of the Unity Party PDCI (Partie Democratique de la Côte d'Ivoire) which was founded in 1961.

The country is divided into 34 political districts (départements) which are named after their main cities and come under the jurisdiction of their prefects. Since the declaration of independence in 1960 Felix Houphouet Boigny has been President. In the last election which took place on October 27, 1985, he ran without an opponent and received 99% of all votes from the people. His political course is strongly western oriented, capitalistic and his basic ideology is a policy of **economic liberalism**.

LANGUAGE

The official language of the Ivory Coast is **French**, which is understood and spoken by a majority of the population. A basic knowledge of the language is necessary, especially if you travel on your own. You can often make yourself understood by mime and gestures. English is spoken only in the major hotels and by students.

Amongst the large numbers of tribal groups on the Ivory Coast there are no fewer than 60 different African dialects and languages. The two most important are **Baoule** and **Dioula**; the last one is considered, in general, as the standard language for trade and is spoken by a large proportion of the inhabitants. If you have a small vocabulary in the language it will be very useful to you at the markets, in families and on the road and will be very much appreciated by the people you meet (see *Appendix*).

ECONOMY

70% of the population of the Ivory Coast lives from the most important economic sector, agriculture, and two-thirds of the agricultural produce is exported.

Since the first cultivation of coffee in 1880 in Grand Bassam the Ivory Coast has become the third largest **coffee exporter** after Brazil and Colombia. The warm humid climate of the rain forest is ideal for the cultivation of cocoa, which has become, next to coffee, the main supporter of the economy.

Bananas, pineapples, rubber, palm oil products and coconuts are other export products from the jungle and coastal regions of the south, the areas most exploited. In the dry savanna regions north of the forest boundary, cotton and sugar cane grow. Millet, cassava, yams, rice, corn and peanuts are grown for home consumption. Stock raising in the north and fishing on the coast serve as a further important food source, although they cannot entirely satisfy the needs of the population.

The export of tropical wood is the most important sources of income for the Ivory Coast. This enterprise together with agriculture threatens the future of the jungle in the coastal areas. Because of this, certain rain forest areas have been designated National Parks and a reforestation programme has begun.

Large **mineral deposits** of gold, diamonds, bauxite, titanium, copper and iron ore are known, but the deposits have not been exploited much. Though petroleum and natural gas are found near Grand Bassam and Jaqueville they do not fulfill the needs of the country. The production of electricity is made possible through power plants along the dammed rivers in the centre of the country.

Industrialization has advanced substantially in the last few years and is dominated by the food and luxury goods industries, wood and textile processing as well as metal production and the electro-technical industry. Abidjan is the most important industrial centre.

Since obtaining independence the Ivory Coast has developed economically quicker and better than many other African nations and the living standard of the population is comparatively high. This economic growth, which is mostly directed through foreign trade, forges strong ties with the western industrial nations. A **liberal economic policy** makes foreign investment easier. Nevertheless, self-sufficiency in food has still not been achieved and the country remains strongly dependent on world market prices of the main exports of coffee and cocoa. This is what made the "Ivory Coast miracle" possible.

Business Hours

Offices and Post office	M-F 8.00-12.00, Sat 8.00-11.30
Banks	M-F 8.30-11.30 and 15.00-16.30
Businesses	M-S 9.00-12.00 and 16.00-19.00

Small shops on the roadsides are often open until late in the evening.

The Country

THE FLORA AND FAUNA

The 550 kilometres of the Atlantic coast to the south is the only natural border of the Ivory Coast. Long palm beaches, divided by cliffs in the west, alternate with wide lagoons and mangrove swamps. The coastal plateau, reaching 100 km inland, is covered by tropical rain forest. Between the dense natural vegetation of giant trees are plantation of bananas, coffee, and cocoa. When travelling north through the countryside into the central plateau you will pass wet savanna with trees and reach broad dry savanna of brush and open grasslands.

Though generally flat, Ivory Coast possesses a wooded mountainous region with altitudes reaching up to 1,200 m in the west, around Man. A multitude of rivers and waterfalls with liana bridges run through this charming region.

The four major **rivers** - Comoé, Cavally, Bandama and Sassandra, run almost parallel to one another water from these rivers is dammed to produce energy. On the northwest banks of the Comoé river the most important of all the eight **National Parks** was established to protect wild animals.

The extremes between the dampness in the south and the dryness of the northern savanna determine the different vegetation zones of the country. Along the coast are large plantations of palm and coconut trees, as well as coffee, cocoa, bananas, pineapples and rubber.

The **equatorial rain forest** bordering these plantations has lost much of its jungle character especially around the built-up areas of Abidjan and San Pedro. Also the many flat areas of fertile soil is used for the farming of coffee, cocoa, bananas, pineapple and rubber.

The **natural tropical forest** with its giant trees, reaching up to 50 m, among them kapok trees, fig trees and parasoliers, whose giant roots rise metres above the surface, can still be found in the National Parks on the coastal regions. Among these, **Tai National Park** in the west preserves some of the last primary jungle forests of western Africa. This dense vegetation offers the animals protection and is the home of chimpanzees, forest elephants, buffaloes, tree snakes, chameleons and a wide variety of birds.

Beach at Assinie ☞

The Country

Bordering the jungle, where the dry period is longer, a mosaic of forest and grasslands unfolds. Deciduous trees replace the evergreens and the leafy canopy is noticeably lower. Characteristic for this region are teak wood, cotton and tobacco plantations. In the extensive, **dry brush and grass savanna** of the north there are fewer trees. Acacia, shady mango trees and bizarre baobab all of which can tolerate the long dry period, characterize the scenery. The river valleys are thickly forested.

The seasonal rain allows for the cultivation of citrus fruit, papayas and sugar cane as well as annual crops of rice, corn, millet, cassava and cotton.

The already largely decimated animal population of the steppe has retreated into remoter areas. The Comoé National Park offers the prerequisites for the survival of antelope, elephant, buffalo, hippopotamus, lion, crocodile, and various species of monkey.

Planning and Preparation

ENTRY REQUIREMENTS/CUSTOMS

British citizens do not require a visa for entrance into the Ivory Coast. A valid passport is needed for a visit of up to three months. American citizens require a visa. Four questionnaires must be completed and sent along with 4 passport photos, a valid passport and the payment fee. A visa extension can be requested at the administrative office in Abidjan responsible for entry permits. When visiting neighbouring countries find out from the consulate or travel agent what visas or vaccination requirements are necessary. The health department also requires an international certificate of vaccination against **yellow fever**.

There is no restriction on foreign or local currency. The following items can be taken into the country duty free: personal travel needs, 2 cameras and 1 cine-camera with film, 1 transitor radio, 1 travel typewriter, 1 pair of binoculars, 200 cigarettes or 250 g tobacco, 1 bottle of wine and 1 bottle of spirits, 250 ml perfume.

ARRIVAL

There are various airlines from western Europe which arrive at Abidjan's international airport, Port Bouet, throughout the week. Information on airfares can be obtained through your local travel agent. Inexpensive charter flights to West Africa also fly to Lomé, Togo and Dakar, Senegal, where you can reach the Ivory Coast either by air or over land. For example, from Dakar by train to Bamako, Mali, continuing by bus to Ouagafougou, Burkina Faso and from there by train to Abidjan.

Direct international flights connect several times a week. Information on flight schedules and prices can be obtained from the national airlines offices.

Air Afrique: Abidjan-Dakar-New York. 01 B.P. 3927, Abidjan 01, tel. 320900, 225531, 226063, 227221.
UTA: Abidjan-Paris-New York. 01 B.P. 1527, Abidjan 01, tel. 332231, 329093.

Pan Am: Abidjan-Dakar-New York. 08 B.P. 392, Abidjan 08, tel. 442132, 368302.
British Caledonian Airways: Abidjan-London: 04 B.P. 827, Abidjan, tel. 321140, 321141.

The airport lies 16 km southwest of the city centre. A taxi to the centre costs approx. CFA 3,000, it is cheaper to travel by the city bus (or the free buses provided by the hotels).

Presently all cross country connections into neighbouring countries are possible. Information of any changes can be obtained from the Ivory Coast Embassy.

Only one passable road is open all year round leading into southern Mali through the border at Pogo-Zégoua. The borders Tiéfinzo-Manankoro and Tengréla-Kadiana are rarely passable in the rainy season.

Entry into Burkina Faso is possible through Ouangolodougou-Niangoloko. The road from Abidjan to Accra, Ghana has just been completed and follows the coast through Half Assinie. Generally speaking the control points are quite thorough and require time; at night the border controls are closed.

Important Addresses
Diplomatic Representatives
Ambassade de Côte d'Ivoire
2, Upper Belgrave Street
London SW 1X 8BJ
Great Britain

Ambassade de Côte d'Ivoire
2424 Massachussetts Northwest
Washington D.C. 20008
USA

Ambassade de Grande-Bretagne
01 B.P. 2581
Abidjan 01

Ambassade des Etats-Unis d'Amérique
01 B.P. 1712
Abidjan 01

Information Offices in Abidjan
Office du Tourisme, Immeuble de la Corniche, Blvd.Gen.-de-Gaulle, Abidjan, 292000
American Express, c/o SOCOPAO, 14, Blvd. de la République, B.P. 1297, Abidjan 01, 323554

MONEY/CURRENCY

The Ivory Coast, together with Senegal, Mali, Niger, Burkina Faso, Togo and Benin, belongs to the **West African Monetary Union**, whose common currency is the **CFA Franc** (Communauté Fiscalière de l'Afrique de l'Ouest).

The exchange rate (2-90) is 1 US$ = 285 CFA and 1 £ = 482 CFA. There are 5, 10, 25 and 100 CFA coins, as well as 1,000, 5,000 and 10,000 CFA bills.

The CFA franc has a constant exchange rate with the French franc: 1 FF=50 CFA. The exchange of French currency into the local currency is therefore very easy. Traveller's cheques (pound or dollar/FF) can be cashed at all banks and larger hotels. Credit cards are seldom accepted and Eurocheques are not accepted at all!

Upon arrival an unlimited amount of CFA francs and foreign currency can be brought into the country (declaration required). Exporting local currency is allowed up to the limit of the amount declared upon arrival or, up to CFA 25,000. Foreign currency control upon arrival and departure usually doesn't take place.

Since the CFA franc is convertable, you can change a small amount into CFA franc before your arrival and upon your return you can convert it back.

When shopping, especially in the markets, there is a constant lack of small change. It is therefore advisable always to carry small change with you.

Planning and Preparation

CLIMATE AND TIME FOR TRAVELLING

The climate in the Ivory Coast can be divided into three areas according to the different vegetation. In the **south** along the coast and in the area of the tropical forests a **humid equatorial climate** prevails. Here the temperatures range throughout the year from 25°-35°C. During the rainy season humidity can reach 90%, difficult for Europeans to adjust to.

This **southern part** of the country has four seasons: From December until the beginning of April is the main dry season, this is the **best time to travel**. The main rainy season lasts from April until July, during which there can be long, continuous rainfall. These months are not suited for a beach vacation, many hotels along the coast are even closed. A shorter dry period in August and September has become less obvious in the past few years. In October and November a short rainy period begins once again. The Gulf of Guinea has a pleasant water temperature of 27°C all year.

In the wooded mountain areas in the west the yearly precipitation, as on the coast, exceeds 2,000 mm. The climate is generally milder with lower temperatures and lower humidity. The rainy season takes place here between July and September. Many tracks are impassable and swollen rivers can become a hindrance. The long dry period from October to May can almost always guarantee pleasant weather.

The **northern savanna region** is similar to the Sudanese climate. Short tropical rain showers which seldom last the whole day occur from June to October. During these months the usually dry savanna is covered with lush green vegetation.

Following this is a long and very hot dry period from November until May. The temperature rarely exceeds 40°C and the nights are comparatively cool. In the months of December and January the heavy *Harmattan* winds arrive, bringing sand and dust from the desert and covering the savanna.

During this dry period a visit to the Comoé National Park is recommended, best at the end of December when the tall grass has been burned off and the animals are easily observed.

The best time to visit the Ivory Coast is between December and May. The farmers leave their fields and the villages are alive with celebrations and festivals with their colourful masks and dances.

Average Temperatures and Precipitation in Abidjan

	Jan	Feb	Mar	Apr	May	Jun	Jul	Aug	Sep	Oct	Nov	Dec
Day	31	32	32	32	31	29	28	27	28	29	31	31
Night	23	24	25	25	24	23	23	22	23	23	24	24
Coast	27	27	28	28	28	27	26	24	25	25	27	27
Rainy Days	4	6	9	11	19	20	12	11	14	18	16	8

HEALTH

Vaccinations

Information on necessary vaccinations can be obtained from your local G.P. At least six weeks before your journey you should have a vaccination plan made out, since not all vaccinations can be given at one time. Some vaccinations only take effect a few days after inoculation. All vaccinations must be registered in your International Vaccination Card with the seal from the Health Department.

Cholera: Since the protection offered by the cholera vaccination is limited and is often accompanied by side-effects, this vaccination is only re-commended for trips to remote areas of the country. In the Ivory Coast it is only required if you come from an infected area. It requires two injections within one or two weeks and provides six weeks protection.

Yellow Fever: Yellow fever vaccination is required. The single inoculation should be given at least two weeks before departure and is effective for ten years. The disease is a virus transmitted by several species of mosquito and can be found throughout tropical Africa. Upon arrival your vaccination card will be checked.

Hepatitis: This illness is often encountered in tropical areas, especially in regions with insufficient hygiene and can be spread through drinking water, food or by contact with infected persons. A vaccination is recommended which is given shortly before departure.

Tetanus: This vaccination is not only recommended for foreign trips, but also at home. Tetanus can be contracted from the smallest wound. The vaccination should be registered in the international card.

Typhoid and Paratyphoid: This vaccination though not required is recommended for all tropical journeys. The vaccine protects for about a year. Typhoid appears under very bad hygiene conditions and therefore vigilance is the best protection.

Malaria-Prophlaxis: Taking proguanil (Paludrine) tablets is the most common protection against this widely spread tropical illness. You must begin one week before your journey and should continue the treatment for six weeks after returning home. At the moment there is no known resistance against Paludrine in West Africa. The symptoms of malaria include weakness, lack of appetite, head and body aches, shivers and high fever. Should you get a fever after your return notify the doctor of your recent stay in the tropics. British travellers should phone the Malaria Reference Laboratory for up to date information: 071 636 7921.

You can protect yourself against mosquitoes, especially on the coastal and jungle regions, by using a mosquito net, often provided in hotels and other places of accommodation. Air-conditioning and insecticide coils can drive away the insects. During walks in the rain forest, in the evenings and at night outdoors you should wear clothing made from tightly-woven cotton material with long sleeves and legs. You should always apply an insect repellent.

Bilharzia

A widely spread illness throughout the tropics caused by infection from small flatworms. These worms spend part of their life cycle as parasites in snails which live in shallow, still or slowly flowing, water or in slightly salty lagoons. Symptoms of the illness include weakness, fever, pains in the upper stomach, blood in the urine. Incubation time is anywhere from four to seven weeks. Avoid swimming in still tropical waters.

AIDS

Reports on this immune deficiency disease can often be heard on the radio and through the media. One thing is sure: Aids is not an "African illness" and therefore the precautions taken at home are the same in Africa- **strictly avoid risks of infection**.

The medical establishment in the Ivory Coast is adequate. In every city and in larger towns you will find a hospital and well-supplied pharmacy. The healthiest person on a tropical journey is one who observes the basic rules of hygiene and health without too much fuss.

It is advisable to visit your dentist at home before the trip and include disposable syringes in your first-aid kit.

General health tips for the tropics

Before your departure you should visit your doctor and dentist for a routine check-up. With regards to your travel plans, they can inform you if there are any additional health risks to consider. If certain measures and rules are observed the risks of a trip in the tropics is not much higher than at home. The first "tropical illness" is often a cold brought on by the change of climate and the air-conditioning in airplanes, hotels and cars.

Don't take on too many major activities in the first days after your arrival; allow yourself to adjust to the new conditions. In the extremely humid climate of the Ivory Coast circulation problems are not unusual. It is most important to drink a lot!!

Sufficient salt intake with meals or through salt tablets compensates for water loss through inevitable heavy sweating. The sunshine in the tropical region is very intense and often underestimated: you should not only protect yourself with some type of head covering and sunscreen (high protection factor) during the midday heat, but also throughout the day.

Unfortunately, in the tropics one is often confronted by annoying diarrhoea which can most often be considered harmless and a result of different diet. Therefore, begin by eating light foods and avoid cold drinks. Freshly prepared meals, well cooked meat, sufficient salt and hot spices (e.g. pimento) reduce the risk of intestinal infection. Water and milk should be boiled for at least five minutes before drinking and you should check the cleanliness of eating utensils.

Should you be afflicted by "Montezuma's Revenge" it is best to drink large quantities of black tea. If the diarrhoea persist, by all means consult a doctor.

Checklist for the first-aid kit
A good supply of medicines you take at home
Malaria tablets
Insect repellents (for the body and coils or sprays)
Pain relievers
Medicines for colds (sore throat lozenges, nose spray, thermometer)
Sunscreens (with high sunscreen factors, lip protectant, After Sun and sunburn lotions)
Eye drops (especially important on dusty roads)
Medicine for nausea and stomach ailments (travel sickness pills),
Circulation tablets
Multi-vitamin and salt tablets
Medicines for diarrhoea and constipation
Water filter or sterilizing tablets
Bandages (gauze and elastic bandages), antiseptic cream, scissors, brush
Plasters in different sizes- you never know when they may come in use.
Disposable syringes

Before departure include a **travel insurance policy**.

LUGGAGE

Suitcase, travel bag or backpack? The type and contents of your luggage depends on, of course, on the type of trip you plan. If you choose to stay in hotels or take part in a hotel excursion, then a suitcase is ideal.

Travel bags or a backpack are easier for carrying on public transport. It is important to choose something robust since your baggage will receive some fairly rough treatment in overcrowded buses, boats and trains. Dirt, clay and oil are less noticeable on dark colours!

On my trip I found a **convertible backpack** the most useful. It can be carried on the back as well as being hand held. It is also easier to open during the many police and military controls. If the material is not water-proof the backpack should be lined with a plastic sheet to protect its contents against the inevitable wet.

For important things such as camera equipment, papers and things which you will need more often during your trip, a day pack or a shoulder bag is indispensable. On public transport it is hard to get to your luggage. In any case, take as little luggage as possible - every bit of extra weight becomes a burden in the humid tropical heat.

Documents

Air ticket, passport, cash, traveller's cheques, driver's license, vaccination card and other important documents should be carried on you (money bag worn around the neck or wrapped around the hips). It is to your advantage to make a **copy** of all your documents and keep them in a separate place.

If you plan on visiting neighbouring countries you will need additional passport photos (when applying for a visa).

EQUIPMENT CHECKLIST

Medicines (see *Health/Travel first-aid*)
Toilet articles, concentrated detergent

Sewing items, safety pins
Rope or clothes line, clothes pegs
Alarm clock, pocket knife
Padlock (for backpack or travel bag)
Torch, spare batteries, candles (in case of power failure)
Photo and film equipment (see *Photography*)

This travel guide, maps, (French dictionary if necessary)
Writing utensils, notebook
Address book, reading material

You can decide for yourself if you want to bring a tent, sleeping bag, cooking utensils, hammock and mosquito net. Since it is quite easy to find, inexpensive and clean accommodation, I don't find these items necessary.

Shops are well stocked and most everyday items are available.

CLOTHING

Clothing suitable for the tropics should be airy, durable, and loose fitting, made from light easy-wash cotton or linen. Long trousers made from tightly-woven material protect against mosquitoes and scratches during jungle walks. Since it can become quite cool in the evening a pullover or sweatshirt should also be packed. In intense sunshine it is best to wear a long-sleeve shirt and hat.

European clothing can be bought almost everywhere, unfortunately it is mostly made from synthetic materials. At the markets you can also find beautiful, colourfully printed cotton material, which can be made up cheaply to your specifications by the market tailor.

On your journey within the country it is best to wear comfortable, light and closed shoes. Well-made tennis shoes or suede leather boots are practical on the dusty, and during the rainy season, muddy roads. Sandals are more appropriate for the beach and the city.

Cheap plastic sandals are available in the markets. They are useful for swimming in the ocean and in hotel showers.

CHECKLIST

Long trousers or skirts, light summer dress, shorts
T-shirts, cotton shirts, blouses (also long-sleeved)
1 sweatshirt or woollen pullover
swimming suit
underwear and socks (cotton)
thin windbreaker and rain gear
2 towels or perhaps a pareo (a large, multi-purpose cotton towel)
scarf or headband, sunhat
good pair of sun glasses
2 pairs of closed shoes, 1 pair of sandals or thongs
money bag to be carried around the neck or as belt

Clothing is an important status symbol in Africa and even people with little means take care to look well-groomed. Appropriate clothing commands respect.

I was once asked by a poor but well dressed student why some tourists he had just seen didn't have better clothing. European fashion plays no role here. It isn't just in office corridors and with host families that a **clean and well-groomed apprearance** is advantageous.

Planning and Preparation

In countries with a predominantly Moslem population, like the Ivory Coast, shorts belong only on the beach. In tourist areas the people have already become used to women in long trousers. In the countryside white women so dressed are likely to be greeted with "Bonjour Monsieur".

In Ivory Coast

TRAVEL WITHIN THE COUNTRY

The road system on the Ivory Coast is among the best in West Africa. Well constructed asphalt roads lead from Abidjan to the north and west, even a multi-laned freeway between the port city and the new capital Yamoussoukro. A coastal road from Abidjan to San Pedro is due for completion in 1990; previously the west coast could only be reached through Gagnoa and Soubré.

Apart from these larger roads, the country is full of many, and for the most part all, weather tracks which also lead to remote villages. Only in the far western region along the border with Liberia and Guinea and in the east on the Comoé river can the back roads become impassable in the rainy season, making any trip more difficult.

The best map is Michelin no. 175 "Ivory Coast" which is quite accurate and up to date. Driving is on the right and French traffic laws are in force.

Those travelling with their own car should enquire before leaving at an automobile club or at the embassy on the state of borders; political changes are often rather sudden in Africa.

Besides the basic auto registration papers you will need a green insurance card, an **international permit** and a "Carnet de passage" (citizen customs declaration) which is issued by the automobile clubs. For your own car or a rental an international driver's licence is necessary.

In Abidjan there are various international car rental agents (Hertz, Eurocar, Avis, etc.) and also the larger hotels within the country offer rental cars. One-way rentals are usually not possible and the driver must be at least 21 years old. Cars of every type can also be rented with a chauffeur. Renting a car on the Ivory Coast is relatively expensive (daily rental about 14,000 CFA plus extras).

There is a sufficient network of petrol stations and in larger cities well-equipped maintenance shops. Those who drive "off the road" should bring with them reserve tanks, spare tyres and all necessary tools. Four-wheel drive is not necessary except in the rainy season.

Outside the main centers traffic is minimal. Since there is the tendency to drive faster on the straight asphalt roads it is necessary to pay attention to trucks and buses.

When possible night driving should be avoided (danger from automobiles without lights).

On the road, especially in areas close to the borders, you will often be stopped by the police or military who will check your papers and eventually your luggage. You <u>must</u> stop, until permitted to continue. Most of the road barricades (against smuggling) are between Man and Odienné in the west (about every 10-20 km).

Public transport is good. Travelling by train, bus or bush taxi is of course more exhausting, but at least you meet people.

Large, relatively modern **overland buses** run according to a schedule (mostly mornings and evenings) on direct routes between the major cities. Neighbouring countries like Ghana, Mali and Burkina Faso can also be reached by bus. Since buses are the favourite mode of transport, reservations and the purchase of tickets in advance is recommended. The tickets are good value, the route Abidjan-Man, for example, costs CFA 3,000 (583 km, 8 hrs.).

Long distances are covered since there are very few stops; there is a break to eat often near a market. The central departure point for trips into the country is the huge bus station in Adjamé in northern Abidjan.

A somewhat more uncomfortable, yet also eventful trip is with the **bush taxi (Taxi brousse)** which takes you on side roads and tracks into the smallest of villages. The bus station (Gare Routière) is often at the market place of a town. There are no set departure times, a bush taxi leaves when all the seats have been taken. The waiting time is often hours. At the station, street urchins, who earn a little pocket money by making arrangements, compete loudly for customers. Check carefully the cost and route, as you may find the taxi does not go directly to your destination.

In Ivory Coast

There are three types of bush taxis: Peugeot 504 (8 seats), Minibus (16 seats) and 'Mille Kilo' (22 seats). If you have the choice of cars when travelling the main routes it is best to choose the smaller, somewhat more expensive Peugeots. They are quickly filled, especially in the early mornings, and they are not held up for long at the different control points.

The prices for bush taxis are firmly set, for every piece of luggage there is an additional fee which is often higher for tourists (bargain!). The best seats are in the front next to the driver or in the larger cars directly in front of the door. To protect yourself from the wind and dust from the open windows a head covering and sun glasses are recommended. On your journey you can stock up with supplies at the markets, you should carry a bottle of mineral water with you at all times.

When taking trips by bush taxi do it in small stages and prepare to be patient, because **flat tyres** are part of the daily routine. During the rainy season the entire taxi service is limited because of the bad road conditions. If there is a lack of taxis you can **hitchhike**, but you will only be taken if you pay (bargain for price!).

The single **train route** in the Ivory Coast is the most important connection within West Africa. It goes from Abidjan north to Ferkéssédougou continuing to Ouagadougou in Burkina Faso. For the entire route of 1,173 km (665 of that in the Ivory Coast) the fast train takes about 20 hours, the express train takes quite a bit longer. These daily trains are comfortable, have first and second class carriages, restaurant and sleeping cars. Reservations are a must.

Example prices: Abidjan-Ferkéssédougou 1st class about CFA 9,100, 2nd class CFA 6,300; Abidjan-Ouagadougou 1st class CFA 19,600, 2nd class CFA 13,800. Sleeping cars cost extra.

Information: RAN, B.P.. 1290, Abidjan, 320245 and at all train stations.

The **state airline** Air Ivoire goes to all important cities either daily or weekly. The prices are very high, a flight from Abidjan to Man costs about CFA 24,100. On the weekends there are reductions of up to 40%.

Information: Air Ivoire, Immeuble Sidam, Ave Houdaille, tel. 323429.

Travel by boat is limited by unnavigable rivers. Occasionally there are boats operating in the lagoons along the coast. Between Grand Bassam and Assinie *Pétrolettes*, small closed motor boats run, and also within the city of Abidjan bus-boats run.

A wonderful experience is the trip from the district of Treichville in Abidjan to Grand Lahou in a *pinasse* across the Ebrie lagoon. The journey lasts about 8-10 hours, and costs about CFA 1,800. Market traders use these simple boats to return to their small lagoon villages.

In all the large cities there are **city taxis**. The price is CFA 100 for every one-way route, except in Abidjan where the taxis have metres (extra at night).

In Abidjan there are buses (Sotra) whose network covers the entire city and the suburbs. The buses run from 5 o'clock in the morning until 1 o'clock at night. The price within the city is CFA 100 per trip.

FOOD AND BEVERAGES

You can find a wide variety of international restaurants for every taste in Abidjan and in the larger hotels in the country. Gourmets coming to the Ivory Coast can truly enjoy eating here as French colonialization has been a positive influence on the food. The culinary delicacies and the French wines in the exclusive restaurants are not exactly inexpensive. There are several Italian, North African, Vietnamese and Lebanese restaurants in Abidjan.

Of course one of the experiences on a trip to West Africa is to become aquainted with the **native food**. Everywhere within the country are typical *Maquis*, simple African pubs where the food, according to region and season, is prepared over an open wood fire. Ask the waiter what is on the menu that day and you can usually choose from two or three meals. A look into the pot can often ease the decision-making.

You can usually eat outdoors in small back gardens. The meals are simple and consist mostly of a **basic staple** such as rice, millet, corn, cassava and yam roots, served with a tasty, spicy sauce made from peanuts or palm oil and fresh herbs. The vegetables include onions, tomatoes, eggplant, okra and cassava leaves. Chicken, fish (the delicious *capitaine*) and grilled or fried meat is also served. Pork is taboo in the Moslem regions.

Often *Viande de brousse* (wild meat) will be recommended, but don't be surprised if along with the small tasty rodents a bit of monkey meat lands in the pot. You should always make sure that the meat is well cooked. Like in other tropical countries you are advised to be careful when enjoying salads, ice cream, and ice cubes in drinks or water.

In African restaurants before the meal the guest is offered a bowl of water and soap to wash his hands. After this a side dish such as Attiété, Foutou or rice formed into small balls and dipped in sauce is served.

It is usual only to eat only with the right hand, the left is considered impure.

You can become best aquainted with eating habits when you have been invited as a guest to eat with a family. This is a special sign of hospitality since food plays a very important role in African life. Everyone sits in a circle and eats out of a common bowl, the guest receives the best pieces.

The following are a variety of national dishes, typical for the country:

Attiéké
This side dish is served mostly in the coastal and forest areas, since it contains steamed cassava flour, comparable to the Arabian *cous-cous*. The very filling Attiéké is served with almost all dishes, mostly with grilled fish and a spicy pimento sauce.

Aloco
Ripe cooking bananas are fried in palm or peanut oil and spiced with steamed onions and pimento. It tastes good with smoked or grilled fish. Aloco can often be found in the food booths at the market.

Foutou
Next to Attiéké, Foutou is the best known national dish and is served as a side dish. A dough is prepared from cooked and mashed bananas and cassava and small balls are formed and dipped in different meat or fish sauces.

To
A simple daily meal made from cassava or corn meal which is mostly served in the African family with gombo sauce, very seldom with meat.

Kedjenou
The tastiest meal of Côte d'Ivoire: A chicken dish served with attiéké or rice. Because of the long preparation time, Kedjenou is seldom offered in a *Maquis*. Here is the recipe which I received from an Ivory Coast family (for 4 persons):

1 large chicken, 2 onions, 3 tomatoes, ginger, 1 garlic clove, 1 bay leaf, pimento and salt.

The cut up chicken is combined with finely chopped onions and peeled and chopped tomatoes, minced garlic and the bay leaf in a pot, seasoned with ginger, pimento and salt, covered and cooked in a medium oven.

Even on longer trips by bush taxi you make numerous stops. Street merchants offer fruits, meat on skewers (brochettes), baked items, fresh French bread and cold drinks. There are also small snack bars at the bus stations in which you can buy omelettes and rice with sauce or an inexpensive breakfast (coffee and white bread, approx. CFA 200).

Mineral water in large plastic bottles ("AWA"), useful on longer journeys. Look out for the original bottle caps. The drinking water which is offered by wandering merchants in refilled bottles and plastic bags is not boiled!

In *Maquis* and hotels very good but strong native beer is served, and in the area around Bouaflé, where the brewery is located, it is available from a keg. A drink typical for the Ivory Coast is *Bandji*, a palm **wine**. It's not served in restaurants, only from markets or as a welcome toast in a village. *Coutoucou*, a homemade, high-proof schnaps can have quite treacherous consequences.

SHOPPING AND BARGAINING

Almost everything that you will find necessary during your trip through the country can be found in the local markets, grocery stores or supermarkets. There is a wonderful tempting collection of **souvenirs**. Art work with centuries old tradition is a speciality of the Ivory Coast. Though you can buy all types of art objects in Abidjan, more authentic and valuable objects can be bought in the country from the artists themselves whom you can watch at work and haggle over the most beautiful items.

Katiola is known for its **pottery**, Bouaké for its beautiful woven **Baoule material**. In the regions surrounding Man you can find typical **sculptures** and **masks** made from exotic wood.

Senoufo in the north of the country, near Korhogo is the centre for ivory carvings. Here too in the villages the famous **hand-woven tapestries** and painted linen scarves with symbolic animal motifs are made. The relief masks made from bronze ("lost wax" technique), bright African material, musical instruments and gold and silver jewellery, which can be made to your design, are all popular souvenirs.

You can get a general idea of the prices at the "Centre d'Artisanat" (sales exhibition), in Daloa, Grand Bassam and Korhogo. Here the government has regulated prices. Generally it is usual to **bargain** over a price, with patience, perseverance and humour! Bargain only when you are truly interested in buying. You can almost always cut the requested price by half, and very often even to a third. An exchange with other objects is seldom accepted anymore in Ivory Coast.

MAIL AND TELEPHONE

The main post office in Abidjan is in the Place de la Republique. It is recommended that letters sent to you be addressed as follows:

M. Smith
Poste Central
Abidjan
poste restante

Côte d'Ivoire

The title Mr. or Mrs. or first names can lead to confusion at the postal storage areas and are better left out.

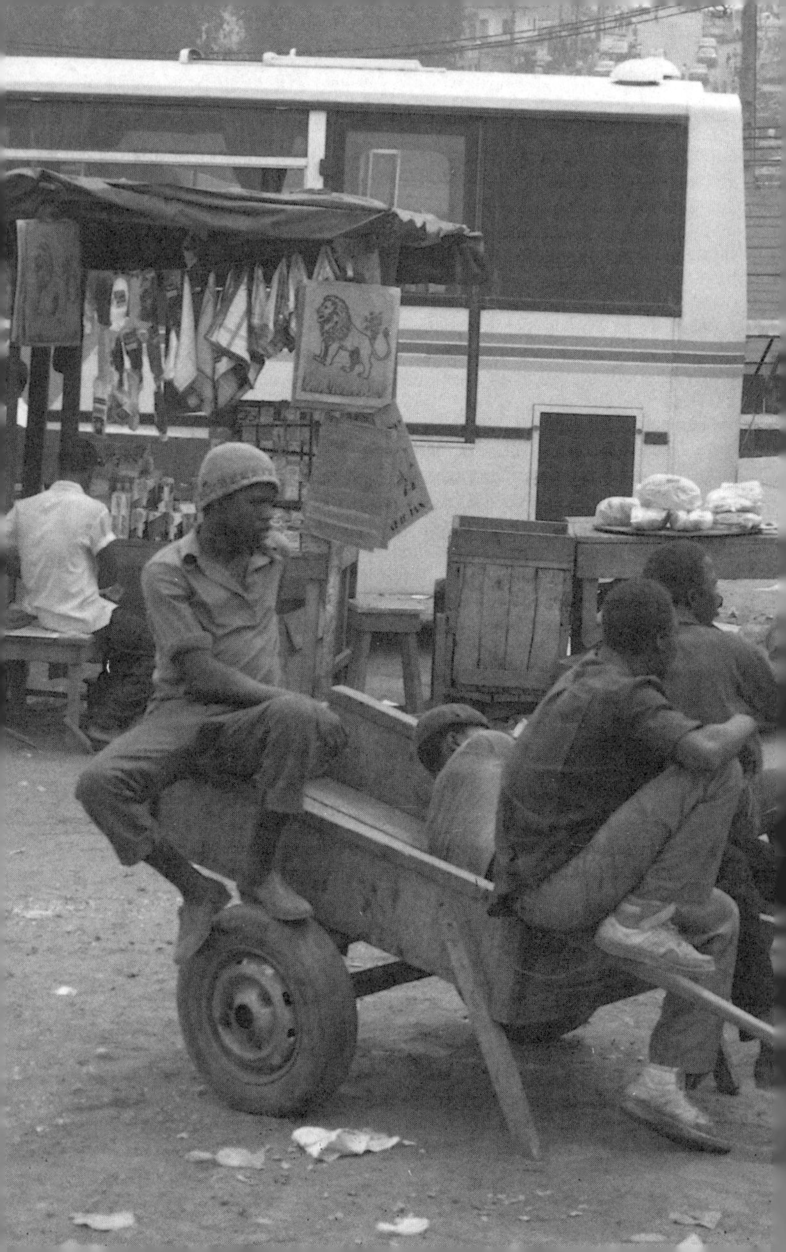

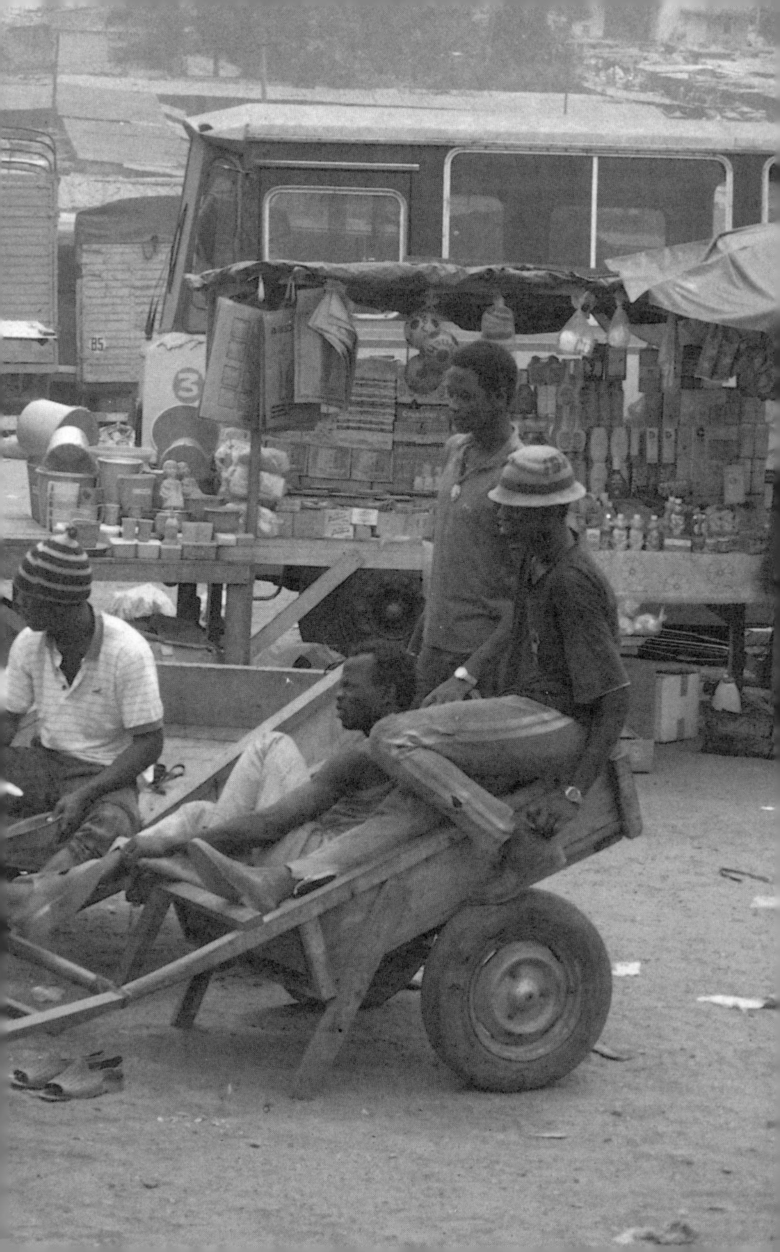

In Ivory Coast

In Africa there is no home mail delivery, rather only P.O. Boxes (B.P.). Correspondence between the UK and the Ivory Coast takes approximately 10-14 days. Postage for a air mail letter (10 g) to the UK costs about 265 CFA.

You can make phone calls in all post offices and from the larger hotels. **International** calls must be placed through the operator, there can be long delays. Only at the main post office in Abidjan can you direct call abroad from the telephone booths. Phoning within the country is not very reliable.

PHOTOGRAPHY

A single reflex camera with telephoto and wide-angle lens offers the best results. An additional small camera proves to be well suited for unexpected snapshots. For museums, craft exhibitions and other dark rooms, a flash is necessary.

To protect against the intensive sunshine and to maintain clear, sharp colours, a polarizing filter is recommended. A small screw driver, lens brush or cleaning paper, lens cap and spare batteries should also be included in your equipment. Old batteries should be replaced with new long-life batteries before the trip.

Most important is to protect your equipment on the road from damp and dust. When driving across dusty tracks in a bush taxi the camera should be wrapped in a cloth and should not be allowed to bump and jolt on the floor. As protection against fine dust particles on the lens a UV or Skylight filter is used. Heat and damp are particularly damaging to film. Exposed film is more sensitive than unexposed film.

Expiry time for a film can already be reduced by one half when the temperature is over 30 degrees. For dry storage a closed film container, an air tight plastic bag and silicon gel, are recommended. You should bring with you the necessary additional film. Film here is not only extremely expensive, but it is also often out of date.

Airport control machines are not always one hundred percent 'film-safe'; a lead-covered bag (film shield) offers safer protection against unwanted damage caused by X-ray machines.

In general you should be discreet with your camera. It is recommended that you use an inconspicuous shoulder bag, which does not give away the value of its contents, rather than a camera bag.

Those who travel on public transport are offered a wide variety of opportunities to take pictures of everyday situations. It is a challenge to take pictures of people, but requires at the same time a large amount of sensitivity. Respect of the foreign culture and observance of religious customs should be more important than the desire to bring home exotic pictures.

Even when the majority of the Moslems no longer consider a photo as strict taboo, you should always ask permission before taking a picture. Certain traditional tribes believe that the evil power of the spirits is drawn out by a camera. Because of this pictures of the rituals and initiation rites of the animistic Senoufos in the north may not be taken. Similarly at the spontaneous mask dances in the west a lot of understanding is needed.

Taking pictures of airports, military sites or police is forbidden.

Strike up a conversation with someone before taking their photogragh, be patient and polite and you'll get good results. Say thank you and be respectful should you receive a refusal. If asked for money or a gift do without the photo session. Often you will be asked for a copy of the picture. A promise to send it from home can bring great joy for somebody. Try to keep your promise.

ACCOMMODATION

You can find luxury and medium priced hotels of international standard in Abidjan, along the coast and in the larger towns in the country. The hotels are not cheap, but you can surround yourself in a little comfort before and after your journey.

There is a wide variety of accommodation throughout the country. In most towns there is a Campement-Hotel (tourist hotel), which, according to its standard, costs anywhere from CFA 6,000-10,000 (double room) per night. Included in the room is a shower and toilet and sometimes air-conditioning; rooms without air-conditioning are cheaper.

There are also numerous "African" hotels, which are very simple, yet for the most part very clean (a shower is almost always available). The rooms are priced between CFA 3,000 and 6,000.

The cheapest accommodation can be found in the so called *Chambres de passage*, which most often consist of a small **bamboo hut** with a bed. There is no electricity or running water, you shower the African way, i.e. out in the open. For such accommodation you pay only CFA 1,000-2,000.

There are no **camp sites** on the Ivory Coast. Camping out in the jungle or on the beach is not recommended (possible theft, etc.)

PART 2

Regional Guide

ABIDJAN

Abidjan, the **most modern city of West Africa** with its futuristic skyscrapers, has been seen as the symbol of the rapid economic growth of the nation. From the once small Ebrie fishing village, a mundane metropolis with about 2.8 million inhabitants has arisen between the branching lagoons and the Gulf of Guinea, ten kilometres away.

At the end of the last century the French captains Houdaille and Crosson-Duplessis discovered this village on a plateau in the middle of the lagoon. It appeared to be the ideal quiet place for a new settlement. An encampment for the French expedition corps was created here.

Its emergence as an important centre was owed to the construction of the railway line Ocean-Niger, which began in 1903. The numerous railway workers settled on the northern peninsula of Adjamé. In 1934 the capital of the French colony was changed from Bingerville to Abidjan and a new administrative seat was created in Plateau.

Twenty years later with the opening of the **Vridi canal** the city became a sea port and its economic development was unstoppable. Although the administrative capital was later moved to Yamoussoukro in 1983, Abidjan has not lost its status as the most important city.

Abidjan has always had a magical power drawing business people from both Europe and Africa. The spacious, expanding port city appeared in their eyes as a dreamland, as a place with many possiblities and opportunities to earn good money. The city, which had 300,000 inhabitants in 1950, is expected to reach 3 million by 1990; an influx which even today Abidjan has trouble dealing with. It is a cosmopolitan city with many contradictions, where mass slum poverty and glass and cement castles exist side by side.

For the inhabitants of the Ivory Coast Abidjan is "like Paris, only more expensive". The sophisticated European lifestyle costs here almost 50% more than in New York, a square metre of land is the highest in Africa.

Plateau

The pulsating centre and heart of the city is the administrative and business area **Plateau**, which is located on a peninsula between Banco and Cocody bays. Here the city builders have created an avant-gard **Manhattan sur lagune** with its modern government buildings, steel and cement palaces, banks, expensive hotels and businesses and at first glance it reminds you of a U.S. metropolis. In this exclusive quarter of Abidjan all threads of the country come together and business is conducted in fully air-conditioned offices.

In the Plateau you can go strolling and shop in exquisite boutiques with the newest *Haute Couture* from Paris, - for those who can afford it. Favorite meeting places for an aperitif are the numerous street cafés where you can flee from the midday sun onto shady terraces and observe the colourful hustle and bustle on the streets - especially the self-conscious and most elegantly dressed women of Abidjan with their artful hairstyles.

The pivot and main business street of the Plateau is the well-loved Boulevard de la Republique. From Place de la Republique in the south this broad, busy and well shaded street passes the city hall (Hôtel de Ville) and continues north past the building of the National Assembly to the Justice building, and just west of that is the president's palace, located in the centre of a beautiful park with a broad view of the Banco lagoon bay.

If you want to go by foot to get a view of this quarter of the city, there are no great distances to cover, but beware of **thieves**, especially on the Houphouet Biogny and General de Gaulle bridges which lead from Plateau into the southern part of the city, Treichville.

Treichville

In this district of the city, which is situated on a lagoon island, you can find the unexpected **contrast** of the truly African heart of the city: A colourful **liveliness** with numerous bars, typical restaurants and markets.

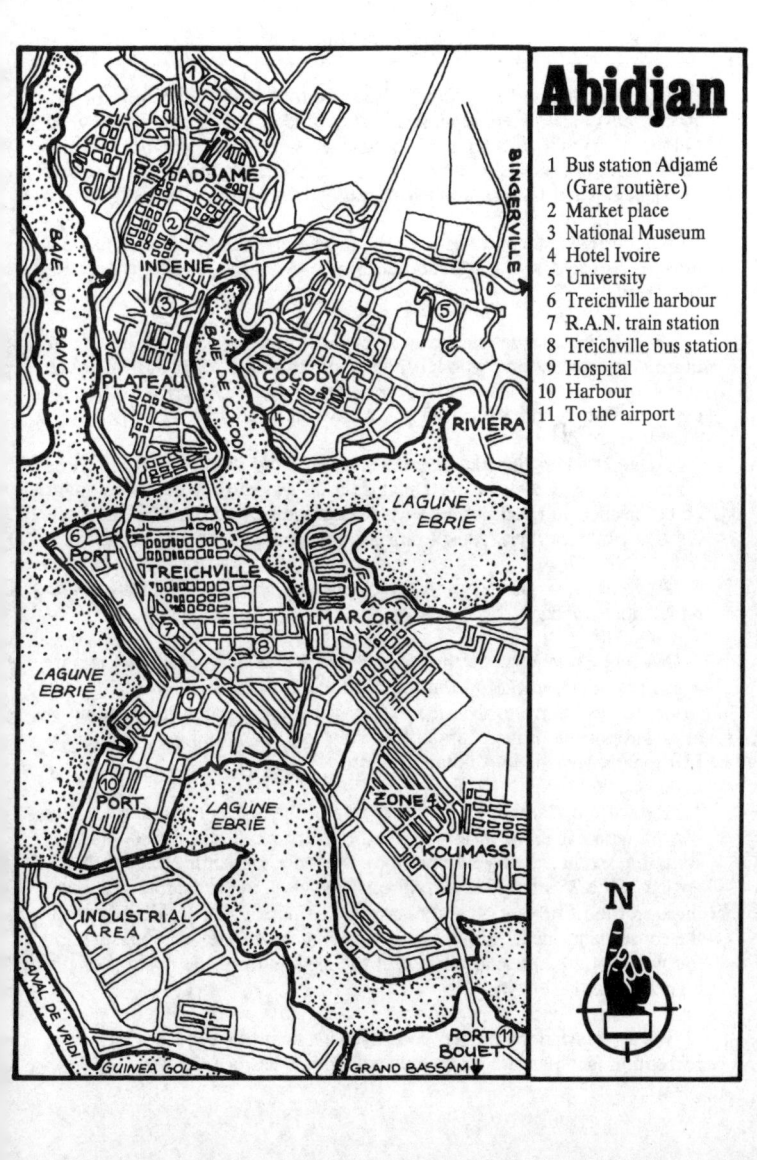

Abidjan

1. Bus station Adjamé (Gare routière)
2. Market place
3. National Museum
4. Hotel Ivoire
5. University
6. Treichville harbour
7. R.A.N. train station
8. Treichville bus station
9. Hospital
10. Harbour
11. To the airport

The central market building draws tourists and the people of the Ivory Coast alike. Here against a background of noises, smells and vivid colours everything is bargained for with passion: brightly patterned material, antiques, crafts, clothing, fruit, vegetables and meat. There are also spicy snacks for sale and rhythmical African music to listen to.

The lively hustle and bustle of the market in Treichville is also a paradise for sticky fingers who should not be given the chance to practise their trade.

Anyone who leaves the main street and ventures into the jumble of aluminium shacks and wooden huts notices that Treichville is a huge slum where people live on the open streets and children have hungry eyes - one of the many dark sides of a city which has grown too quickly.

At night when the Plateau seems to be dead then Treichville turns into a **"red light district"**. At nightfall life awakens in the many night clubs, casinos and restaurants with African music and dancing. In these districts of the port city prostitution continues to increase.

Anyone who wants to go to Treichville at night should definitely take a taxi, never walk.

West of Treichville, on the banks of the Ebrie lagoon is the large port area of Abidjan, further to the south is the industrial area. When driving from the city centre to the airport you will come through the residential area **Marcory** with its distinquished villas and beautiful gardens. Most Europeans working in Abidjan live here.

East of the Plateau, on the other side of the bay, is the green **Cocody** district with exclusive residences and university. If you are looking for someting exotic, then you can enjoy the only ice-skating rink in black Africa in the 25 storey Hotel Ivoire. This hotel, in the middle of a huge park on the Ebrie lagoon and almost a city in itself, is considered one of the most luxurious in Africa and is certainly worth seeing. Certainly for the wonderful panorama offered of the skyline from the rooftop of the highest point in the city.

Further east along the **African Riviera** a beautiful suburb with hotels, recreation facilities and an 18-hole golf course has been created.

Abidjan City Center

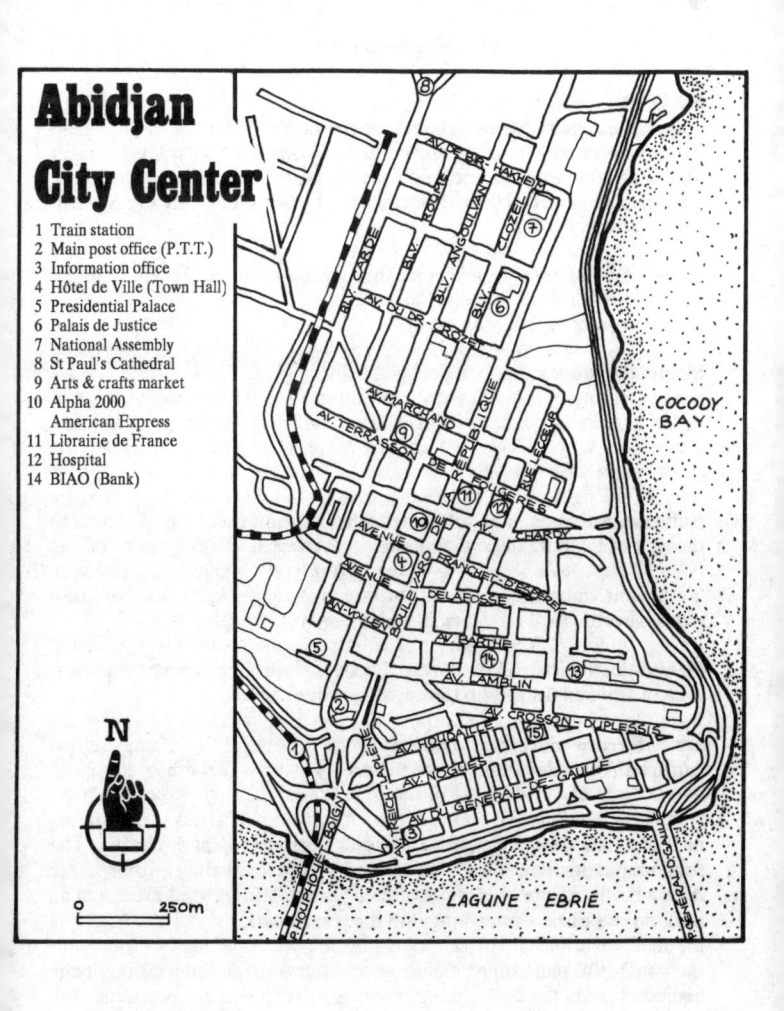

1 Train station
2 Main post office (P.T.T.)
3 Information office
4 Hôtel de Ville (Town Hall)
5 Presidential Palace
6 Palais de Justice
7 National Assembly
8 St Paul's Cathedral
9 Arts & crafts market
10 Alpha 2000
   American Express
11 Librairie de France
12 Hospital
14 BIAO (Bank)

Adjamé

Adjamé, a typical African quarter in the north of the city, is similar to Treichville in that it too has kept its lively market and colourful night life. It also retained its former village character: a jumble of small houses and huts, divided by earthen streets, a motley ethnic mixture from all over the Ivory Coast.

The unimaginably large central bus station is the focal point of life in Adjamé. Buses and bush taxis leave in all directions and into neighbouring countries from this point.

Sights to See

Being a young city Abidjan does not offer many obvious sights, most of the old colonial buildings have been modernized or pulled down. Therefore, a short stay, either before or after your journey in the country, is usually enough.

National museum: The ethnological collection gives a good view into the cultural inheritance of the over 60 different ethnic groups of the Ivory Coast: traditional woven and batik crafts, gold work, symbolic masks and statues, copper and bronze figures, ceramics and furniture pieces are on display. Behind the museum in the park is the **national library** building. The museum is situated in the northwest part of the Plateau at the end of Boulevard Carde. Hours are (except Monday) 09.00-12.00 and 14.30-18.00, admission is free.

Art and crafts market: The market in the centre of the Plateau across from the Alpha 2000 building is mainly for tourists and offers almost all types of arts and crafts from different regions of the Ivory Coast, but also from Mali, Burkina Faso and Ghana. Apart from nicknacks you can find beautiful wooden sculptures, musical instruments and cloth. The predominately Senegalese traders are hard bargainers, things are definitely cheaper at the Treichville market. You can, at any rate, get an idea of the prices before going into the countryside.

St. Paul's Cathedral: Already visible from a great distance this huge cathedral stands on the corner of Av. Terrassonde Fougères and Boulevard Angoulvant. The futuristic architecture, designed by the Italian Aldo Spirito, involved immense construction costs. The official opening was made by the Pope in August 1985.

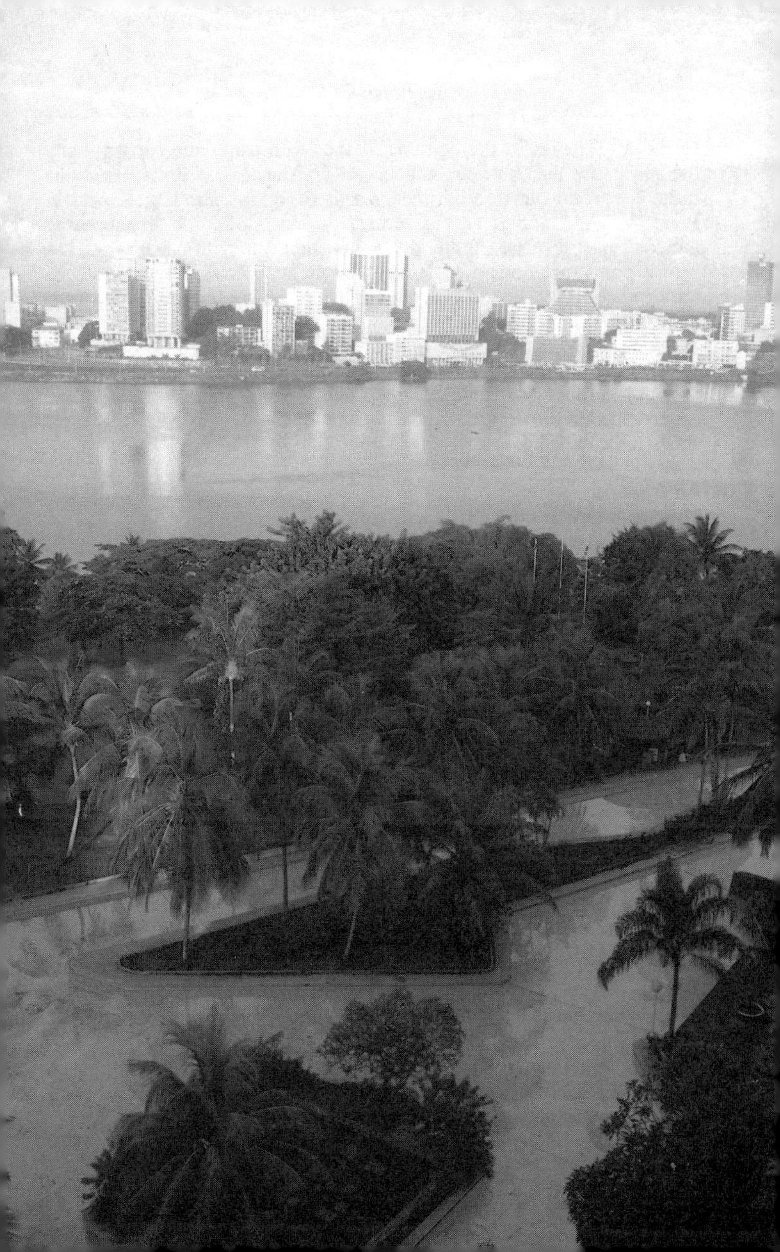

Harbour: Thanks to the opening of the Vridi canal and consequently the navigable link between the ocean and lagoon, 90% of economic trade is carried out through the port at Abidjan. The largest port in West Africa, it serves as the central docking point for neighbouring nations, and because of the rail connection 'Abidjan-Niger' it is the transit point for goods going into the Sahel countries. Apart from its importance to the oil refinery it is a major fishing harbour. The port authorities offer guided tours.

Another worthwhile visit is to the hotel restaurant 'Wafou' which is on Boulevard de Marseille designed like a **village on stilts** with straw-covered round huts on the lagoon. Expensive, but worthwhile; folklore show in the evening.

Addresses
Tourist information: Office du Tourisme, Immeuble de la Corniche, Boulevard Géneral-de-Gaulle, tel. 292000.

Travel agents: Afric-Voyages, Ave. Chardy, tel. 332951.
VT 2000, Blvd. Clozel, Immeuble GYAM, tel. 227671.
SOAEM Voyages, Rue du Senatrur la Garof, tel. 327503.
SOCOPAO Voyages, Immeuble Alpha 2000, Ave. Chardy, tel. 228384.

Hospitals: Hospital de Cocody, tel. 439024.
Hospital de Treichville, tel. 369122.

Pharmacies: Pharmacie Central, Franchet d'Esperey, Plateau, tel. 327964.
Pharmacie du Plateau, Immeuble Botreau-Roussel, tel. 331764.
Pharmacie du Grand Marché, Treichville, Place de l'Ancien Marché, tel. 222728.

Banks: BIAO, Ave. Joseph Anoma, Plateau, tel. 320722.
Banque Central des Etats de l'Afrique de l'Ouest, Rue le Coeur, tel. 320466.
SGBCI, Immeuble Air Afrique, Ave. Joseph Anoma, Plateau, tel. 320335.

Book store: Librairie du France, Ave. Chardy, Plateau, tel. 321321. City maps, French language travel guides and good African literature.

Regional Guide

Main Post Office: Place de la Republique, Plateau. Open Mon-Fri 07.30-12.00 and 14.30-17.30, Sat. 07.30-12.00. Direct overseas calls can be made from telephone booths here.

Hotels

Abidjan has a number of luxury hotels belonging to international hotel chains, e.g. Hilton, Novotel, Intercontinental, etc. all very expensive.

Here is a list of medium priced hotels and inexpensive lodging in the different city districts.

Plateau

- Hotel Ibis Plateau, 7 Blvd. Roume, B.P. 1185, medium priced hotel in the administrative centre of Plateau with 190 rooms, a restaurant and bar; tel. 320157.
- Hotel des Sports, Ave. General-de-Gaulle, B.P. 455. Simple, clean and inexpensive lodging in central location; across from Novotel, whose swimming pool can be used free of charge. Surroundings (Quartier de commerce) are practical for shopping purposes. Terrace bistro. Room with shower/WC and air-conditioner approximately CFA 6,000-8,000, also cheaper rooms without air-conditioning and with WC on each floor, tel. 327137.
- Centre d'Acceuil Missionaire (C.A.M.), 23, Blvd. Clauzel (across from St. Paul's cathedral), clean, and simple lodging. Normally reserved for missionaries and their friends; if there is room, here is inexpensive lodging, tel. 331619.

Treichville

- Hotel de France, 19 Blvd. de Marseille. About 3 minutes by foot from the railway station in Treichville. Older, but well kept hotel, 50 simple and clean rooms with terrace bar. Relatively inexpensive, tel. 325618.
- Hotel International, Autoroute de l'Aéroport, B.P. 1763. A bit loud, but clean and inexpensive hotel with 52 rooms, the cheaper ones on the street side. About 300 m from sport facilities, close to restaurants, night clubs and bus station, tel. 321085.
- Hotel Terminus, Blvd. Delafosse, B.P. 790. Across from the railway station in Treichville, ideal for visits to the harbour and the markets. Studios with kitchens and air-conditioning, medium priced, tel. 321198.
- Hotel Haddad, Ave. de la Reinke Pokou, right next to Hotel Terminus. One of the least expensive hotels in Abidjan, rooms are approximately

CFA 3,000, there are no comforts, it is a bit noisy and has occasional water problems.

Marcory
- Hotel Hamanieh, Blvd. de Lorraine, B.P. 548. Quiet medium priced hotel close to the residential area, 84 comfortable rooms.
- Hotel Ibis Marcory, 4 Blvd. Giscard d'Estaing, B.P. 594, tel. 369255, international medium priced hotel, 140 rooms, restaurant, swimming pool. Convenient location close to the airport, tel. 369155.

Adjamé
- Hotel du Nord, Face de l'Agence Hachette, Quarter '220 Logements'. It has a convenient location near the bus station and close by are small African restaurants; 34 rooms with shower/WC. Pleasant, well kept and clean, tel. 370463.

Restaurants
There is a wide variety of restaurants to choose from in Abidjan including everything from French luxury restaurants with *Haute cuisine* and all types of foreign specialities to simple, inexpensive Maquis. You can get the best tips from the local people. However, here is a list of restaurants in which you can eat typical African dishes.

Marcory
Le Varican, behind Hotel Monapi, near the church of St. Therèse. Beloved Maquis. Lovely roof terraces which are lit up at night. Somewhat touristic, but wonderful Ivory Coast specialities. Recommended is the *poulet braisé* (grilled chicken).

Plateau
- Climbié, at the corner of Av. Chardy and Rue Lecoeur, high class African restaurant, air-conditioned.
- Marhaba, Boulevard Lagunaire, wonderful North African dishes.
- Maquis 'Guichet 23', Place de la Republique near the main post office, good Ivory Coast food.

Treichville
- Chez Babuya, Rue 7/Ave. 7. Only open evenings, Mauritanian specialities: Doves with dates, Lemon Chicken, Cous-Cous, a bargain.
- Chez Mamie, Immeuble Sicogi Arras, Rue 38, African specialities.

- Le Calalou, Avenue 2/Rue 6, dishes from Togo.
- Marrakech, Av.21/Rue 13, Moroccan cuisine.

Zone 4
- Santa Maria, Blvd. de Marseille, very nice location, directly on the lagoon, seafood specialities. Reservations are recommended.
- Maquis Chez Mado, Rue Calmette, very good dishes from Cameroon, inexpensive.

Along the coast (Zone Cotière): Chez Cakpo, Blvd. du Canal Vridi, crawfish and fish specialities, very good African cuisine.
- Restaurant de Plage, Chez Tonton Marcel, Grand Bassam, Ivory Coast specialities (Kedjenou, kebabs) and fish dishes. Not exactly a bargain.

In comparison to that you can eat rather inexpensively at 'le Bar du Marché', Plateau near the market - cheap French menu. And in 'Les Retrouvailles', Blvd du Gabon, in the Marcory district, there are excellent kebabs and good music.

Night Clubs
There is an especially large selection in the city district of **Treichville**. The best known night clubs are 'la Canne à Sucre', the 'Boule Noire' and 'Treich-Can-Can'.

Swimming Pools
For a small fee you can use the swimming pools in the larger hotels without being a hotel guest. The use of the swimming pool at Novotel, Ave. Général-de-Gaulle, Plateau, is free of charge.

The prettiest swimming pool is the Disneyland pool at Hotel Forum Golf, Riviera district, where you can swim between islands, small waterfalls and bridges. The entrance fee is high, as at the Hotel Ivoire, whose swimming pool is in the form of a huge lake and surrounds the entire hotel complex.

Traffic Connections
From the airport
Between the airport, Port Bouet and the Plateau district are the bus routes 6 and 29. Since most of the international flights arrive or depart around midnight it is advisable to take a taxi.

Although the taxis in Abidjan have meters you will be required to pay a special tarif on the route from the airport to the city centre, which increases after midnight. Do not take the first one, rather do a little bargaining for a better price which should be around CFA 2,500 for each trip. For tips and taxis it is a wise idea to have already exchanged a small amount of money into CFA-Francs at home.

Your first night in a hotel should be booked, if possible, from home before you leave, especially in the tourist season.

In the city
The green buses with the letters SOTRA are quite inexpensive. A one-way ticket within the city costs CFA 100, in the outlying areas and to the airport CFA 125. The buses run around the clock, the central departure station is the Place de la Republique. For long trips you can rent a city taxi on a daily basis.

Train
The railway station for route Abidjan-Ouagadougou (RAN) is in Treichville. For information and time schedule ring 322066.

Travel by boat
Moorings in Treichville near the Houphouet Boigny bridge. From here you can travel with busboats between the city districts of Yopougon, Plateau and Treichville.

You can take longer trips over the lagoons with a *Pinasse* to the towns of Assinie, Jaqueville and Grand Lahou. On Sundays and holidays there are boat trips from the mooring at Plateau. Departure times: 09.00, 11.00, 14.00. On such excursions you can get a good impression of the lagoon city. For reservations and information ring 321796.

Bus stations
Adjamé, the largest bus station on the Ivory Coast where buses and bush taxis leave for all over the country, Mali and Burkina Faso. Since the many different departure points are hard to understand in the hustle and bustle, it is best to take a taxi to the station and ask the driver to find your bus. Treichville: Departures for Grand Bassam, Assinie, Aboisso. For buses to Accra, Ghana there is one single S.T.C. bus station (State Transport Cooperation) on Boulevard Delarosse.

Regional Guide

Some distances
From Abidjan to

Yamoussoukro	245 km
Comoé National Park	746 km
Korhogo	635 km
Man	573 km
Grand Bassam	43 km
Aboisso	118 km
Abengourou	210 km

NEAR ABIDJAN

The Banco National Park

Just 3 km northwest of the city limits of Abidjan is a 3,000 hectare jungle protected as a National Park since 1953. The lush green scenery with its huge trees and tropical plants and the Banco river running through it, offers a relaxing change from city life. On the shore of the lake on the jungle limits is a small restaurant. Unfortunately it is only opened at weekends, offering typical African dishes. You can reach the Fôret du Banco best by taxi which you can use throughout the excursion. Walking through the rain forest is not recommended because of the danger from bandits. It is interesting to watch the launderers spread out their brightly-coloured cloth over the fields and rocks beside the River Banco.

Plage de Vridi

At the southern limits of the city, not far from the airport, palm rows stretch along the Vridi beach. At weekends the people swamp this near-by recreation area. Because of the strong breakers swimming in the ocean is not possible; this is true of the entire east coast. Accommodation can be obtained in the elegant Palm Beach Hotel (354216) or less expensive - Hotel Grillon (355260) under the coconut palms. On the beach there are excellent restaurants serving seafood specialities.

EAST OF ABIDJAN

Grand Bassam

Just a half hour's drive by car from the busy and lively centre of Abidjan takes you back into early colonial history. The first **French trading post**

Ghanaian Fishing Harbour in Sassandra

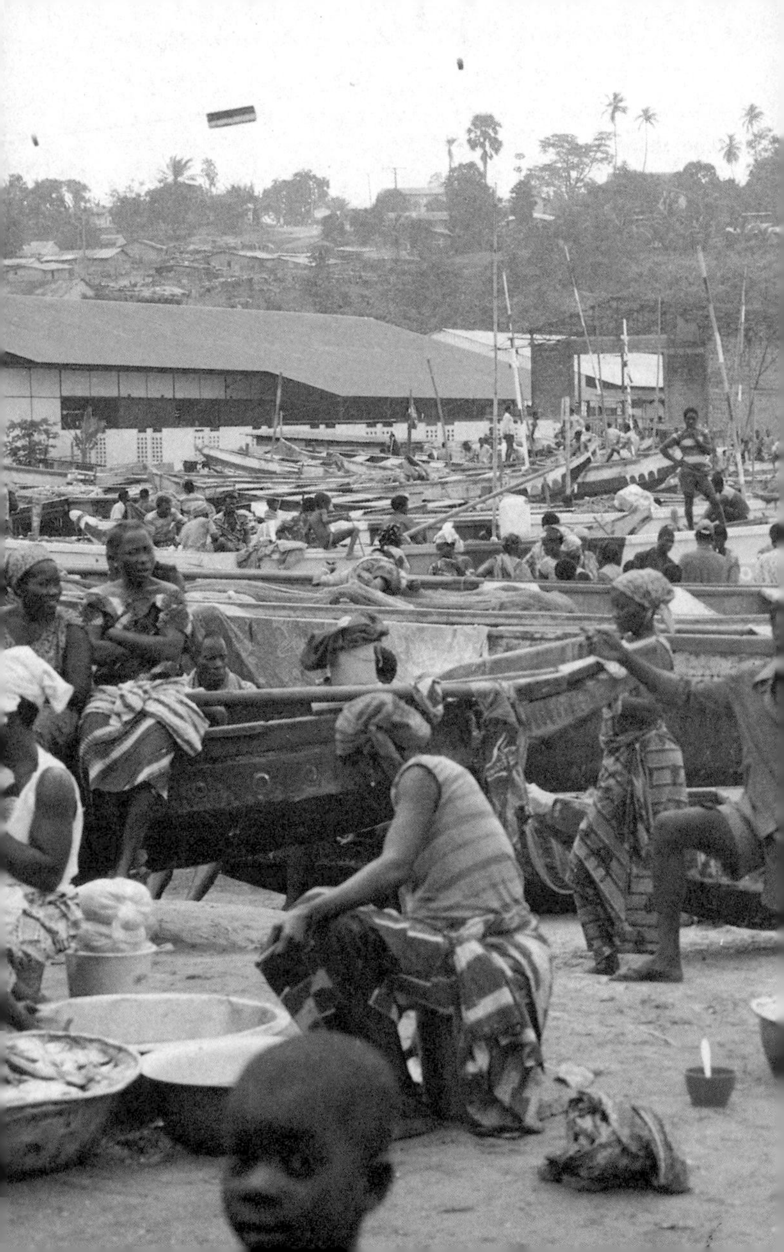

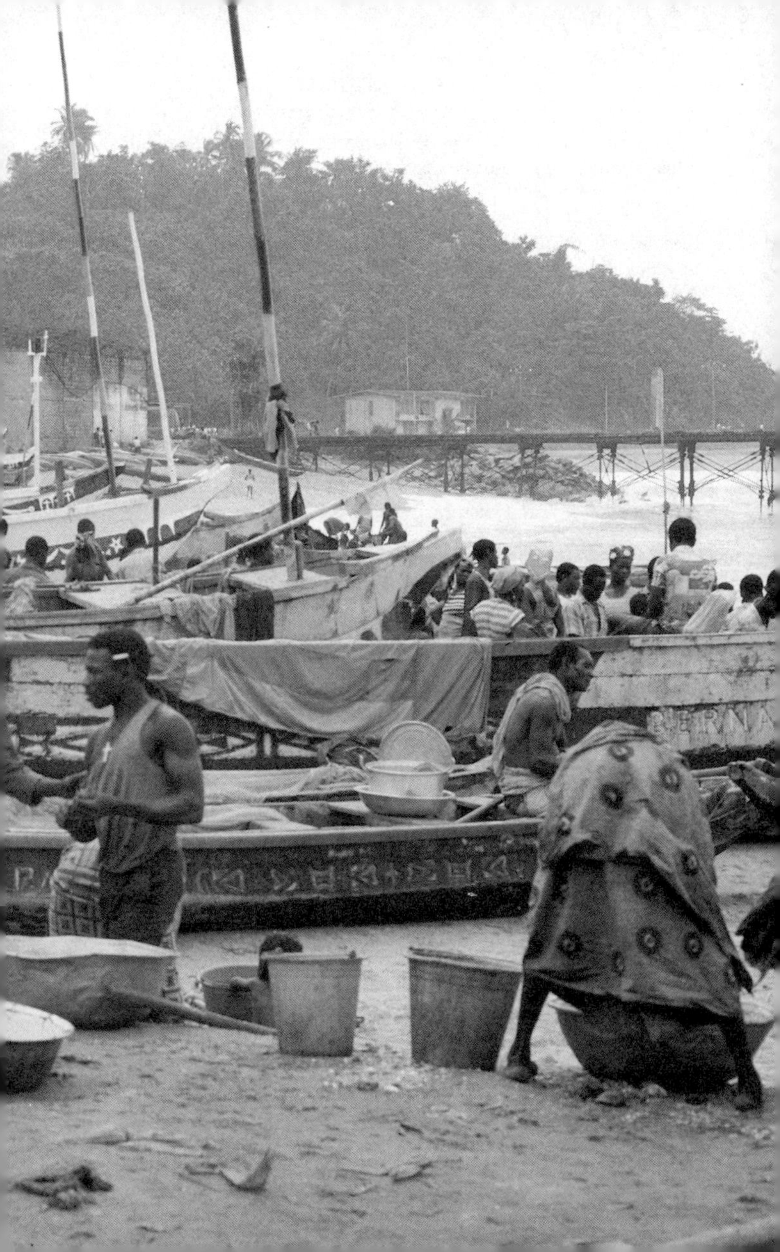

was located here at Grand Bassam, the mouth of the Comoé river, between the lagoon and the ocean.

In the year 1842 a famous treaty was signed between the French lieutnant Fleuriot de Langle and Grand Bassam's village chief Atekeble in which the settlement was ceded as a French protectorate for a mirror, a weapon, three cases of whisky and a barrel-organ. The first trading houses were built and in 1893 Grand Bassam was declared the capital of the French colony.

Just a few years later, in 1899, a sudden plague of yellow fever forced the Europeans to transfer the capital to Bingerville. Only nostalgic ruins of the magnificent manor houses with their columns, arches and wooden balconies, now overrun by tropical vegetation and left abandoned, remain from this glorious time. Today the sleepy, almost ghost-like town is the most interesting historical site of the Ivory Coast.

You can reach this old town on the ocean from the bus station by going through the market and over a lagoon bridge. Turning left you are on the way to the earlier **governor's palace**, which was renovated and made into a costume museum in 1980.

Along the deserted street you will pass the old **palace of justice**, **prison**, a church and the well-kept market halls. At the bend in the road is an interesting small pottery shop where you can observe craftsmen at work. The street ends at the mouth of the lagoon where fishermen work from their *pirogues*.

From the bridge, your starting point, you can reach the European cemetery in the west. The beautiful road along the ocean leads through palm plantations and further into the small fishing village of **Azuretti** with typical huts made from palm branches.

Besides the interesting history of Grand Bassam there is another tourist attraction: the wonderful, **palm lined beaches**, when people from Abidjan want to turn their backs on the overcrowded city at weekends they relax here in small straw huts beside the ocean. Fortunately only a few hotels have been constructed whose palm covered bungalows blend in well with the scenery. As I have said, the heavy seas along the this coast do not allow for swimming in the ocean.

When life on the beach becomes too one-sided, you can explore the lively small market, go fishing in the lagoon or visit an arts and crafts centre. Every year in November Grand Bassam celebrates a a week-long, colourful, traditional 'Abissa' festival, when the N'Zima tribe honour their dead.

You can reach Grand Bassam from the bus station in Abidjan-Treichville where at short intervals buses and Peugeot 504 bush taxis leave along the 43 km asphalt covered road. Shortly before Bassam various souvenir and craft shops occupy both sides of the road.

Accommodation
- Assoyam Beach Hotel, 20 air-conditioned rooms, restaurant, swimming pool, and the most expensive hotel in Grand Bassam, tel. 301557.
- La Taverne Bassamoise, 15 air-conditioned rooms, swimming pool. Known for its excellent, but expensive restaurant, tel. 301016.
- Le Wharf, very informal, small hotel with 8 rooms, shower/WC, fan. Simple, clean and inexpensive (cheaper rooms in the back building): terrace restaurant, tel. 301533.
- Chez Antoinette, very cheap private rooms, near the 'La Paillote', not directly on the ocean.

Assinie
With its wonderful white sandy beaches under coconut palms, its heavy breakers on the ocean and the quiet mangrove-lined lagoon, Assinie is one of the most exciting **vacation areas** on the Ivory Coast.

In this paradise-like **tropical scenery**, on a narrow piece of land between the canal of Assinie and the Gulf of Guinea are located two exclusive hotel villages: 'Club Méditerranée', with bungalows in the Sudanese style, swimming pool, night club, and folklore and the club village 'Les Palétubiers'. There is a restaurant and swimming pool in the middle of a tropical garden, and many sport and excursion possiblities in the lagoon.

There are also cheaper alternatives: At weekends many small *pailottes*, simple palm straw huts, can be rented on the beaches.

By car from Abidjan it takes about two and a half hours on a good asphalt road (80 km) to the village of Assinie from where you follow a track to the small beach village Assouindé on the peninsula of the lagoon. From Grand Bassam take a bush taxi. Also city taxis from Grand Bassam can bring you on a day excursion. The chauffeur must have a police permit. Since this road goes on into Ghana there are many controls along the way.

If you have plenty of time you can travel from Abidjan or Grand Bassam with a *pinasse*, a small trade boat, over the canal to Assinie.

Bingerville

15 km beyond Abidjan on Route de Cocody you will come to the small village of Bingerville, named after the explorer and captain Louis Gustave Binger. The trip along asphalt roads goes by palm groves, avocado and pineapple plantations and over small hills where you can get a good view of the surrounding area.

This town on the **Ebrie lagoon** has a very pleasant climate, it is understandable why the French moved their colonial capital in 1900 from Grand Bassam to Bingerville after the yellow fever epidemic. A memorial to this time is the well-kept **governor's palace** which is presently used as an orphanage.

The **botanical gardens** are worth seeing. They were planted in 1912 with typical flowers and trees from the region. Half way along the road that leads to the lagoon is the *École d'Art Africain*, a school for African sculpture. More interesting than the school itself is the attached **Combes Museum,** named after the French sculptor Charles Combes (free admittance). Huge sculptures from tribal artists are on display here.

Bregbo

Only a few kilometres from Bingerville towards Eloka, is a road turning right which goes to Bregbo, a small Ebrie village. It is the residence of the **prophet Atcho**, an unusual healer and preacher of the Harrist sect. His art of healing is based on an old form of psychotherapy. In conversation the reasons for the spiritual illness is explained and apparently in 90% of all cases is cured with a mixture of healing herbs. Albert Atcho enjoys the complete confidence of his followers, many of the patients remain in the village whose only street leads to the Harrist church and to the prophet's residence.

Aboisso

Aboisso can be reached by bush taxi from Abidjan via Grand Bassam along a 122 km asphalt road. Because of its excellent location in the Abi lagoon, Aboisso was made into a **trading post** by King Louis XIV of France in the 17th century.

For a long time trade was conducted here with the Karawans from the north. Today the small city is the departure point for excursions into the beautiful surroundings. In a *pirogue* you can go along the Bia river passing wooded islands and hilly scenery as far as the Ayamé reservoir on the Bia dam.

If you are an adventurer and love secluded areas you can try a trip to the north in a 'Mille Kilo' or truck along the former Karawan road. The difficult track, which passes numerous small villages and goes through beautiful forest areas, ends in Abengourou 182 km later.

Accommodation
Hotel Bemesso offers clean rooms with showers and fans, approximately. CFA 3,000.

THE WESTERN COASTAL REGION

A long island of sand east of the city of Fresco divides the ocean from the many lagoons, which continue from 300 km to the border with Ghana. While swimming here is hardly possible because of the heavy breakers and strong current, there are rock cliffs west of Fresco which calm the sea and make swimming possible, for example at the beaches near Sassandra, San Pedro Grand Bereby.

Broad **palm beaches** alternate with picturesque bays and tropical forests, in which tiny fishing villages hide. There are few possiblities for accommodation near the beach.

Jacqueville
When heading west from Abidjan towards Dabou, after 35 km you will reach the road junction where the ferry crosses the Ebrie lagoon. The crossing - for cars too - lasts about 20 minutes and on the other side a newly constructed road runs along the promontory between the ocean and the lagoon to the small coastal village of Jacqueville.

From the Adjamé bus station in Abidjan there are bush taxis which run daily to Jacqueville (11 km); from Treichville there is a trader boat which goes through the Vridi canal via the lagoon.

When the first Europeans reached this villge, they met a tribal group which had emigrated from Ghana in the 16th century. The British established an important trading post here which at that time was called Grand Jack. Later it became **a centre for the slave trade to America.** It was in 1878, upon the arrival of the French, that the city received its present name. In contrast to Grand Bassam, here you will hardly be reminded of the town's moving history, only a few dilapidated colonial houses along the coast remain.

The wonderful palm beaches are the true attraction of the small, quiet town which stretches along the lagoon strip to the mouth of the Bandama river. Despite the closeness of Abidjan there are not many tourists, only at weekends do a few explorers come, mostly to fish. Swimming in the ocean is only recommended for very competent swimmers. Excursions in a *pirogue* through the mangrove swamps or a visit to small fishing villages in the area is an alternative to relaxing on the beach.

In September each year, the Harrist prophet Papa Novo celebrates at a huge festival in the village of Toulouzou, 30 km away.

Accommodation
- Hotel M'koa, away from the ocean on a small lake, a modern hotel with 22 air-conditioned rooms, restaurant, night club and swimming pool. Expensive!
- Campement hotel, only a few minutes walk from the bush taxi station situated on a beautiful palm beach. Run by Swiss. Small, straw-covered round bungalows with shower/WC, Open-air restaurant.

Ile de Tiegba
This is an interesting village on the western edge of the Ebrie lagoon. The coastal inhabitants live in simple huts constructed from twigs on stilts in the lagoon, and their diet is mostly fish. A *pirogue* trip through the village gives the feeling that time has stood still. In the last few years, however, more fishermen have moved to solid land where they can use electricity and have water supplied in their new houses.

The journey begins from near the Adjamé railway station in Abidjan in a Peugeot 504 bush taxi stopping at Dabou. From this point 'Mille Kilo' run at irregular intervals several times a week to Tiegba. It is more reliable, however, to use a taxi in Dabou.

Check the car and the tyres before you leave, because this track is in very bad condition.

Accommodation
'Aux Pilotis de l'Ebieye': simple hotel built on stilts with four rooms, near the mooring. From the terrace there is a wonderful view of the lagoon. Here you can also inquire about *pirogue* excursions.

Grand Lahou
There are daily bush taxis which run from Abidjan to the coastal town of Grand Lahou, 142 km away. The trip itself is very interesting, you can get a good view of the different plantations and crops of this region.

The asphalt road ends at Dabou and a relatively bad track leads the last 98 km to the coast. At the end of the track you cross the Tagba lagoon by ferry (free of charge) and come to Lahou-Plage on the promontory.

Other travel possibilities between Abidjan and Grand Lahou is by *pinasse* (trader's boat). The departure is from Abidjan-Treichville, mostly at night, and can take up to 10 hours, since the boat stops along the way in many small lagoons.

Grand Lahou (Plage) is situated on a narrow piece of land between the ocean, a quiet lagoon and the mouth of the Bandama river. The town was founded by the British and the Dutch until the French made it into an important trading, customs and postal station in 1890. Today, only the neglected colonial houses covered by bougainvillea and shaded by coconut trees are reminders of this boom period in history. An almost ghost-like atmosphere remains in this quiet paradise, far from civilization.

When leaving the mouth of the river, passing the old residential area and administrative buildings, in the village, you come to the market hall which was built in 1930.

A small track runs along the ocean and leads to the European cemetery and the abandoned mission with its well-kept Catholic church. Another 2 km and you come to the large residential area of the Avikam, who live here in huts built upon sand and who lead a very peaceful life.

Next to them a few traders and fishermen from Benin and Ghana live among the ruins. Though attempts were made to deport them they have refused to move.

In 1975 the entire administration of the town was moved 17 km inland and a new, modern Grand Lahou II was founded. It was feared that the ocean would soon destroy the promontory.

Accommodation
- Campement Hotel in a beautiful location at the tip of the promontory at the mouth of the Bandama river. Small round huts with WC/showers, mosquito nets, restaurant, double room about CFA 8,000.
- Chambres de passage, in the middle of town, inquiries can be made at the old market hall. Simple **bamboo huts** (no electricity, no sanitary facilities), about CFA 1,500.

Surroundings
From Campement Hotel you can use the hotel motor boat for fishing in the lagoon, excursions in the mangrove swamps, trips to chimpanzee island or to the **Azagny National Park**. This 30,000 hectare jungle preserve has hardly been developed for tourism and can only be reached by boat and by foot.

The thick forest area is home to a variety of birds, buffalo and a few of the last elephant herds in Ivory Coast. They can be observed from sight-seeing plateaus or - somewhat more expensively - by means of a sight-seeing flight in a private airplane.

In the area around Grand Lahou **swimming is very dangerous**.

Sassandra
A trip on asphalt roads takes you from Abidjan, through the wooded region beside the coast to Divo. Those who want to stop here can find inexpensive lodging (room CFA 2,000) in Hotel Relais (near the Total petrol station). After the junction in the road near Lakota, a bad track

runs first over the Sassandra river, then south through the exciting landscape of thick rain forest, coffee, cocoa and coconut tree plantations. The many small **mud hut villages** along the way seem to be totally untouched by the 20th century.

The first impressions of Sassandra might be a shock - dusty, sleepy and picturesque houses from the pioneer period are situated on green hills between the mouth of the river Sassandra and the Atlantic. At the end of the 19th century the French had founded an important trading point here. In 1951 it became one of the most important centres on the west coast.

However, Sassandra became a victim of the renovation of the large port at San Pedro further west: the landing stage, storage silos and the port office are all closed. The only thing that remains is business carried on in the fishing port where the Fanti fishermen, originally from Ghana, offer fish for sale every morning from their colourful dug-out canoes.

The prettiest view of the city can be seen from the church or from the prison peninsula directly at the mouth of the river. Most of the the inhabitants of Sassandra are quite happy with life here, which seems to be cut off from the rest of the world. However, it is not without its problems: a large number of the Néyo living here are unemployed and the city lacks sufficient water and petrol supplies.

But Sassandra does not want to be forgotten and has now dedicated itself to tourism. On both sides of the city there stretch endless palm beaches with small bays which are lined with cliffs rising up from the ocean. At the moment there is only one beach hotel.

Arrival
358 km on tarred roads from Abidjan, or 98 km on a rough track from San Pedro. Daily buses run from both cities and bush taxis run from Sassandra. Several times a week there are flights from Abidjan, which occasionally land in San Pedro, and from where 'Mille Kilo' operate.

Accommodation
- Campement Hotel, on the beach. From the bus station turn left along the street which runs beside the ocean towards the prison. Large rooms with shower/WC, about CFA 8,000/double room.

- Hotel Grau, older and simpler hotel directly behind the bus station, rooms for CFA 3,500. Restaurant and grocery store available.
- Hotel de L'Ouest, on the north road out of town, older hotel with some air-conditioned, simple rooms, about CFA 3,500 occasional water and electricity problems. Excellent food and very friendly owner, who also offers small straw huts 3 km further along the beach.

Surroundings

By *pirogue*, you can cross the mouth of the Sassandra river and reach the beautiful beaches near Trepoint, east of the city.

Along a track, past the airport, through the palm oil plantations and tropical forests you come to the small fishing villages of **Niezeko, Lateko, Labléko, and Poliplage**. They are situated on a fantastic, lonely palm beach where the ocean is calmed by a small reef and whose only activity seems to be the arrival and departure of fishermen.

To reach here take a taxi from Sassandra (e.g. trip to Poliplage about CFA 4,000 per car), the taxi driver will pick you up later at a designated time.

San Pedro

San Pedro can be reached by bush taxi from Abidjan on a 480 km long asphalt road via Gagnoa or - quicker, several times a week, by plane.

This town, built from nothing in 1968, has the atmosphere of a **satellite town**. The houses are randomly distributed and growth is hindered by the surrounding swamps. Here, on a drawing board, the second largest port in Ivory Coast was planned. Guest workers from neighbouring countries and people from the centre of the country displaced after the creation of the great **Bandama dam** were moved here.

Although the port has grown, but not as much as was hoped, it remains in second position after Abidjan.

Because of the stagnation in development many people have moved on. The majority of those who have stayed live now in poor wooden plank huts in a huge **slum**, called the 'Village'. A large part of the forest area around San Pedro has been felled.

The large, market in the middle of this slum area is worth a visit. To search for the city centre of San Pedro will be in vain, the individual districts are so far apart that you can only reach them by taxi. Perhaps the situation in the city will change when the coastal road from Abidjan, now under construction, is finished.

And yet San Pedro is charming and the people a delight. The wonderful beach 'Balmer Plage' with small typical *paillote* restaurants under the palm trees is situated on the coastal road behind the port area.

Accommodation
- Hotel Atlantique, rather old, well cared for in colonial style, about 1 km from the beach. Rooms with air-conditioning, shower/WC, about CFA 8,000.
- Hotel Climbié, clean, small African hotel in Sewek Quarter I, rooms with or without air-conditioning CFA 2,500 and 4,000 respectively.
- 'Le St. Tropez', on the coast road beach, restaurant and beautiful camp site, tents available, CFA 2,000/night.

The only beach hotel available is 'Balmer Plage' in a wonderful location just west of the city, presently under reconstruction.

Surroundings
Approximately 4 km west of San Pedro is **Pointe Taki**. In the shadow of the promontory is a totally protected bay: a **swimming paradise** for water sports fans.

The beach at Monogaga, 50 km east of the city, can only be reached over a very bad track. Among lush vegetation, fine sandy beaches and along cliffs washed by the quiet ocean is one of the most beautiful beaches of the Ivory Coast, close to the small, sleepy fishing village of Grand Béréby.

Grand Béréby
The promontory of Béréby and its beautiful beaches can be reached by bush taxi on a 59 km long track from San Pedro through forest, coconut and rubber plantations. On one side is a bay with *filaos* (type of conifer) protected by cliffs where a quiet ocean offers safe swimming. On the other side of the peninsula is a rugged palm beach with high seas. The native fishermen who fish from their *pirogues* have recently gained a new

source of income: at the tip of the promontory a luxury hotel has been built bringing tourism to this small fishing village.

Accommodation
- Hotel Baie des Sirenes, bungalows, shower/WC; swimming pool, open-air restaurant, large selection of sport facilities. Double room approx. CFA 50,000. Excursions in a *pirogue* and to the Tai National Park. Private airplanes from Abidjan also possible, tel. 711520, information at Africvoyage Abidjan, tel. 332951.
- Hotel Mani, very simple, clean, African hotel in village, rooms about CFA 3,000.

Small *Maquis* offering inexpensive African dishes are easy to find.

Tabou
Small town in the southwest close to the border with Liberia and offers very little for tourists. Tabou is 81 km by bush taxi from Grand Béréby through the coastal forest. The route south from Guiglo along the Tai National Park and Liberian border is unreliable.

Very few bush taxis travel from village to village in this region though there are occasional trucks. Nevertheless this track is especially interesting for its unique landscape and settlement.

Because of its isolation Tabou feels as if it is at the end of the world. The beaches are deserted. You will meet loggers transporting huge tree trunks to the port on over loaded trucks on washed out roads.

The southwest is the homeland of the interesting **Kru** people, who in small family groups dedicate themselves to fishing and agriculture. East of the city you can find lodging in a small campement hotel on the beach.

Boubélé
Boubélé, 25 km from Tabou is a small, typical fishing village where the Fanti fishermen, originating from Ghana use brightly decorated *pirogues*. Boubélé slumbered for a long time until a bungalow village was erected on the beautiful, lonely palm beach at the mouth of the Houo river. Accommodation is in comfortable rooms with air-conditioning: the *paillote* restaurant on the beach is known for its good food. The hotelier offers excursions into the surrounding area.

Boubélé is the ideal place for all those who love isolation, though a stay there will not be cheap. (approx. 18,000 CFA/room and board) Information: Travel Agent VT 2000, Abidjan.

About 10 km south of the village **Ménéké** (on the road to Tabou), is a gorgeous beach, not far from Boubélé, which definitely deserves an excursion. Here you can rent simple grass huts for CFA 1,000. Similar huts are also available in the village of Toulou, about 10 km west of Boubélé, for CFA 1,000.

THE CENTRAL REGION

This is the area of transition between rain forest and savanna in the heart of the Ivory Coast. Humidity is much lower than in the south. The scenery changes gradually, the forest becomes more open and divided by numerous streams. Further to the north it turns into **humid savanna**, dotted with bushes and trees.

In 1972 a dam was built on the Bandama river to produce electricity. This drastically changed the scenery in the north and drove people from their land. The central region is the homeland of the **Baoulé tribe**, which, along with its 15 sub-groups, represents the largest and most significant tribe in the country. They cultivate the fertile land, but are unable to raise cattle because of the continued presence of the **Tse-tse fly**.

Yamoussoukro

Approximately 270 km from Abidjan along the only multiple-lane highway in the country is the new (1983) **administrative capital** of Ivory Coast, Yamoussoukro. In only a short period of time this once small village, the birth place of the head of state, Houphouet-Boigny, has grown into an African 'Brasilia' and has no equal. Gigantic buildings in extravagant achitecture dominate the land-scape, four-lane highways come from nowhere and end in the wilderness. At night street lamps light up deserted areas. On the edge of the avenues rural Africa encroaches; familiar piles of grain and clothes are left to dry.

The **Party House** is situated on a hill, surrounded by parks. Somewhat further is the most splendid hotel in Ivory Coast, Hotel 'President' with its swimming pool of marble and one of the most beautiful golf courses. The elegant town hall, modern banks and school buildings stretch out to the bus station and the market.

The most impressive building is undoubtedly the **Basilica of Our Lady of Peace**, the second largest cathedral in the world, surpassed only by its model, St Peter's in Rome. Built at enormous expense the basilica can hold 20,000 people in its air-conditioned interior. It was opened by the Pope on September 10,1990. The other religions building is the great **mosque**.

Despite all the advances made, Houphouet Boigny has allowed African myths to liven up his ultra modern city: **Holy crocodiles** (afternoon feedings) romp in water ditches surrounding his palace in the north of the city.

Accommodation
- Hotel 'La Residence' at the northern exit to the city, medium priced hotel with air-conditioned rooms, bar, restaurant, night club, about CFA 10,000/double room, tel. 640048.
- Hotel du Paysan, directly opposite the bus station, simple and somewhat neglected, rooms from CFA 7,000, tel. 640031.
- Hotel Confidence, near mosque, across from the cinema. Inexpensive accommodation, simple and clean.

There are numerous motels with restaurants at petrol stations near the bus station. Recommended: Mobil and Esso, prices range from CFA 8,000.

Surroundings
In the nearer vicinity are Houphouet Boigny's huge state plantations. Using the newest experimental methods, coffee, cocoa, yams, avocados and rubber are grown on model plantations. Heading north through the plantations you reach Kousso, the huge Bandama reservoir dam. It has an area of 1,700 km^2 almost three times as large as Lake Geneva. Behind the 1.5 km long wall a track leads to a hill where there is a wonderful view of the lake.

Bouaké
380 km north of Abidjan is the **second largest city** and important trading and transport centre. Situated on the main north and south junction on

the only railroad connection in the country, it is the transition point between forest and savanna.

Tribes from almost all parts of the Ivory Coast mix here with the Baoulé residents and give the city its lively, busy character. Bouaké is economically significant because of its **textile industry**, the oldest factory was built in 1919.

The main point of attraction is the huge market in the centre of town where the Dioula trade and sell. Besides food and crafts from all over the country, many different materials are on sale. Baoulé material is very famous, also indigo scarves and cotton material in an endless variety of colours and patterns. The cultural high point for the Bouakés is the **carnival** which takes place for a week in March, involving decorated carts, music and dance.

Accommodation
- Hotel Harmattan, 633995, and Hotel RAN, 632016, two very comfortable hotels in the upper price list in a central location.
- Le Provencal, older, very clean hotel with cosy atmosphere, nice terrace restaurant, about CFA 8,000/room , 633491.
- Hotel Iroko, 633495, on Avenue Houphouet Boigny, fairly new, inexpensive hotel.
- Hotel Tianya, near the water tower and 700 m from the sports stadium, inexpensive.

Very inexpensive lodging can also be found in the youth hostel, as well as the Protestant and Catholic missions.

Katiola
From Bouaké, 55 km north along the main road is the small city of Katiola. For tourists the **women's pottery workshop** is of interest. Traditional hand-made crafts can be found near the Hotel Hambol, and modern ceramic work can be found at the pottery school in the town centre. The craftsmen, who can be observed during the week at their work, expect a tip.

In December the **hunt for agoutis** (a rabbit-like rodent) takes place. This speciality is excellently prepared in the Ghanese restaurants on the road to the station.

Accommodation
- Hotel Hambol, comfortable hotel, upper price bracket, tel. 654725.
- Hotel Makarwa, simple and cheap hotel in the centre of town.
- La Paillote, clean round bungalows, quiet location, 2 km from city centre.

Bouaflé

The small quiet town of Bouaflé, 59 km from Yamoussoukro, is well suited for a stop over on the way west. Dirt roads, simple living areas, the wooded surroundings, the lively market and bus station give the town a very typical character. Beside the road, besides everyday items, are some interesting things: traditional fetishes, dried monkey hands, reptile skins, stuffed birds, teeth and bones from jungle animals - all endowed with their own magic.

Accommodation
Campement Hotel, located at the northern entrance to the town, small informal hotel, very quiet. In the restaurant you can eat excellent *Cous-Cous*. The patron, a Frenchman, loves conversation and organizes excursions in the **Maraoué National Park**, not far away, whose beautiful savanna landscape (100,000 hectare) contains very few roads. The game population is limited. The buffalo, monkeys and antelopes that inhabit the area are rarely seen except in the early hours.

Daloa

Through virgin forest and plantations an absolutely straight asphalt road leads from Bouaflé to Daloa, 82 km away. The city is a crossing point of many routes and offers very few tourist attractions. At the town entrance is a small craft centre where you can observe carvers. Gold ornaments are relatively inexpensive and can be made in a short time according to your wishes.

Accommodation
- L'Auberge de l'Ouest, at the bus station, tel. 782090.
- Hotel Brinqué, near the market, friendly and quiet, about CFA 5,000.

THE WESTERN REGION

The western region of the Ivory Coast near the border with Guinea and Liberia is one of the most exotic areas of the country with its jungle,

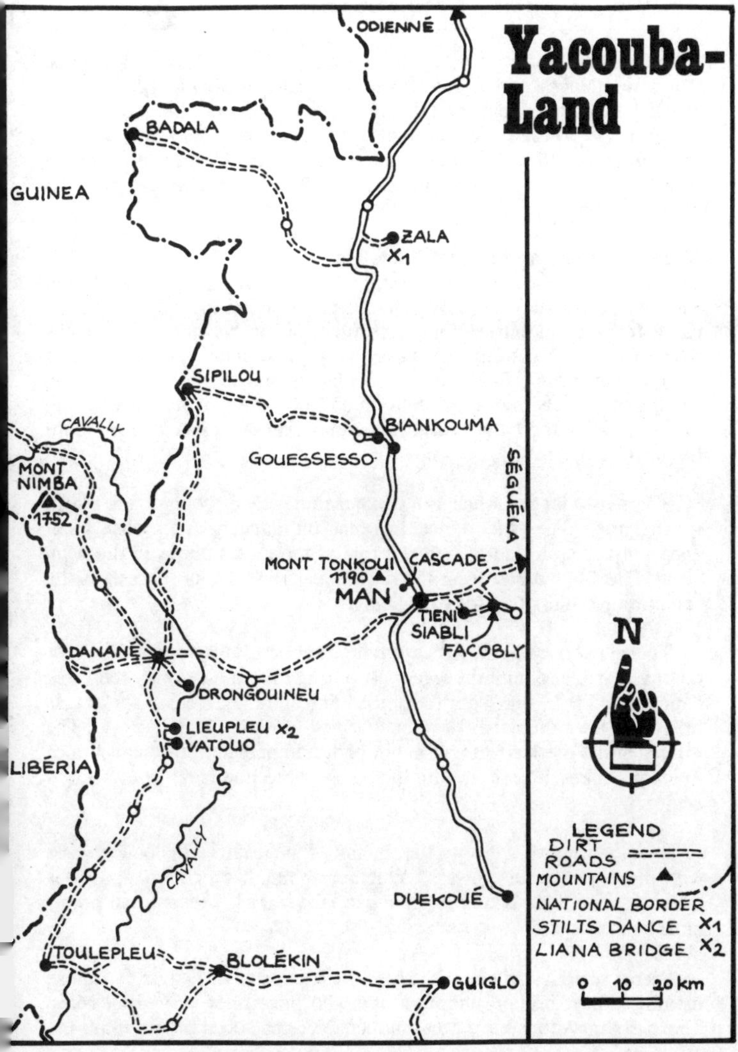
Yacouba-Land
ODIENNÉ
BADALA
GUINEA
ZALA
X1
SIPILOU
CAVALLY
BIANKOUMA
GOUESSESSO
SÉGUÉLA
MONT NIMBA
1752
MONT TONKOUI
1190
CASCADE
MAN
TIENI
SIABLI
FACOBLY
DANANÉ
DRONGOUINEU
LIEUPLEU X2
VATOUO
LIBÉRIA
CAVALLY
DUEKOUÉ
TOULEPLEU
BLOLÉKIN
GUIGLO
N
LEGEND
DIRT ROADS
MOUNTAINS
NATIONAL BORDER
STILTS DANCE X1
LIANA BRIDGE X2
0 10 20 km

rivers, water falls, mysterious liana bridges, ritual masks and dances. The mountainous region ascends in the vicinity of Man to 1,200 m and reaches its highest point of 1,752 m at **Mount Nimba**. Because of this range the region has a comfortable and somewhat cooler climate than the humid south. The best time here for travel here is between September and May; during the ensuing rainy season there can often be endless tropical rain showers.

Masks, Dances and Secret Societies

The mountainous region in western Ivory Coast is the land of the **Yacoubas**, also know as **Dan**. This large ethnic group, which originally came from neighbouring Liberia, settled on the banks of the Cavally river in the 14th century. Although they came under the influence of many other tribes, they have been able to maintain their language, traditional beliefs and a **symbolic mask cult**. In comparison with the other masks of the Ivory Coast the famous Dan mask has its own, more human character.

The mask dances, which are conducted mostly by young men, play a special role. The **stilts dance**, in which the dancers accomplish great acrobatic feats on 3 m tall stilts, is one of the most famous in the Man area. The **Goua dance** from the region near Biankouma represents the celebration of initiation for young men.

The villagers gather together on different occasions, such as births or deaths, marriages, initiations, harvest or disputes, and through the mask dances ask for favour from the spirits, ancestors and gods. The masks first come alive after they have been called from the 'Holy Forest'. The wearer of the mask covers his entire body and puts himself into a trance to identify himself entirely with the being whose power he would like to acquire.

In an expressive dance to the rhythm of the drums a dialogue is held with the supernatural powers. Whether animal-like or human, serious or comic, one thing is true of all masks: the secret of their ritual power must be preserved.

Secret societies still exist today in the Yacoubas or Dan tribe, whose members must remain unknown and who must obey very strict rules. These organizations have great influence on the social order within the tribe and mediate in the case of disputes. The members of a secret society possess the ability, so it is said, to change themselves into animals. Here the leopard possesses the most power. In case of serious crimes the society can decide to poison the guilty person.

During your travels you might meet young girls whose faces are decorated with kaolin. This is a sign of the recently completed circumcision ceremony which takes place before marriage. The circumcision of girls has become rare in our time, but for each young man it remains a requirement before being accepted into adulthood. In the villages large mask festivals celebrate the end of the initiation and ask for the gods' blessings.

The Cowrie Shells
In the 18th century Dioula traders imported from the Indian Ocean a small white shell, the cowrie. Up until about 60 years ago this shell was the method of payment between the tribes of the Ivory Coast.

Today the cowrie shell decorates traditional garments and masks in the west and north of the Ivory Coast. As a symbol of the female sex it is used by young girls as head jewellery, especially during celebrations.

The Liana Bridges
The liana bridges (made from the woody vines) in the land of the Yacoubas in the west of the Ivory Coast are famous and woven with tales. The people of Yacouba land keep the decorative construction of the liana bridges as a secret.

In one single night, so it is said, the banks of rivers and ravines are connected with the decoratively knotted net of thin and thick lianas. The ends of the bridges, hanging from dizzying heights, are often fastened to branches which are only as thick as a finger.

Nobody is able to look on or even ask about certain details when the 'initiated' are at work. Those who do it nevertheless, risk their lives! The work can only be completed in such a short time due to the help of the spirits and under the protection of masks.

You must go barefoot over the swaying bridges, the lianas are holy and shoes are considered sinful.

Man

The district capital of the west has a special attraction, thanks to its exotic location in a valley surrounded by mountains. The city itself with its streets full of pot holes, does not offer many sight-seeing attractions. Most interesting is the large covered market in the centre of town, the meeting point for traders and buyers who exchange news and goods. On the upper floor of the market interesting artwork from the region is sold, among them beautifully woven cloth and the sought-after Dan masks. The **ivory** which is seen here originates from central Africa, hunting on the Ivory Coast is strictly forbidden: do not buy it!

Arrival

You can reach Man by an Air Ivoire flight from Abidjan several times a week. Express buses also run between Man and Abidjan; departures mornings and evenings (advanced reservations are recommended); price for one-way ticket CFA 3,000. 583 km, about 8 hours driving time, eating stop at Yamoussoukro.

Numerous bush taxis connect Man with Biankouma, Odiénné, Danané and other small villages in the area. With a 'Mille Kilo' you can reach Bamako in Mali over the Tengréla border (recommended only in the dry season since the tracks are very bad).

Since there are five different *gares routières* for buses and bush taxis, it is best to inquire when you get there about the one you want. The bus station for Danané and Biankouma is located next to the mark-et in the centre. Taxis within the town cost about CFA 100 per route.

Accommodation

- Hotel des Cascades, most comfortable hotel in town, situated on a hill above the market. Restaurant, bar, swimming pool (entrance fee CFA 700, if not a hotel guest), tel. 790252.
- Hotel Beauséjour les Masques, outside the town on the Route d'Abidjan. Round bungalows with straw roofs and decorated with local paintings in a quiet garden. 38 well furnished rooms with air-conditioning, shower/WC, from CFA 5,000, tel. 790991.
- Hotel Leveneur, central, a few minutes from bus station, near the Maquis Paillote. Very simple rooms with shower, CFA 5,000 (a bit loud).
- Chez Tanty Akissy, Quartier 13, behind the stadium. Simple, clean hotel, from CFA 3,000, tel. 790478.

- Hotel C.A.A., quite new, cheap guest house, clean rooms with shower and fan, CFA 3,000. In Quartier 13 behind the hospital and below Hotel Cascade.

Restaurants
- Maquis La Paillote, nice, somewhat touristy in an inner garden covered with palms next to Hotel Leveneur. Mainly European food; African speciality: *Kedjenou*. Not exactly cheap. Simon, the French patron, also manages the bar at the cascades and the Hotel 'Les Lianes' in Danané.
- L'Univers and Le Tirbo, two typical *Maquis* with inexpensive Ivory Coast dishes, where you eat under the open sky.
- Tanty J'Ai Faim, Quartier Avocatier. Paillote restaurant where small African dishes are prepared in the open.

Area Around Man

From Man there are numerous possibilities for excursions into the surrounding area, thanks to its extremely exotic scenery, interesting cultural and traditional background and the ritual masks and dances. These sites can be reached by bush taxi, and organized tours with a guide are offered from various travel agents and from 'Hotel des Cascades'.

A six km walk will lead you to the **cascades**, the stair-like waterfalls in the middle of the tropical forest, which, however, are only full during the rainy season. The liana bridge which leads over the river has long been destroyed and it is uncertain as to when it will be renewed.

There is a track (20 km) which leads to the top of **Mount Tonkoui** (1,200 m) west of the city which offers a wonderful panoramic view as far as neighbouring Guinea. In the upper region of the mountain **cinchona** has been planted, and the vegetation is lush. Shortly before the summit there is a waterfall.

13 km east of Man is the small village of **Tieni-Siably**, which is also easy to reach by bush taxi. On the top of the cliffs stand the last round huts of the old village, whose history reaches far into the past. The oldest person of the village (said to be 110 years old) lives here; of his 36 wives only one is still alive. Before climbing the cliffs you should introduce yourself to him. The old man likes to tell stories of Tieni and its legendary cliffs. Also noteworthy is the ancient **'Holy Tree'**.

For hiking fans a climb up the **Dent de Man**, 14 km northeast of Man and the symbol of the city, can be recommended. When leaving Man along the road to Séguéla, after 2 km a left turn leads to the village of Gouapoloulé. From there difficult tracks lead to Glonguin. Make yourself known to the village chief and he can find a guide for you. The climb (about 6 km) is tiring and the path itself is not easy to find. Good shoes are a must!

In the vicinity of the village of **Facobly**, 22 km east of Man, with a little luck, you may see hippos and crocodiles. The village is located in the middle of wooded mountains on the banks of the Sassandra river and is also particularly known for the 'Tematé' dance at rice harvest time.

Danané
Near the small town of Danané, 79 km west of Man and not far from the border with Liberia, is a beautiful **liana bridge** which goes over the Cavally river. For those who have no vehicle of their own, Danané can also be reached by 'Mille Kilo', although the track is in a bad state! From there you can take a bush taxi in the direction of Lieuplue getting out at the junction shortly before the town. You can reach the river and bridge on foot along a 6 km track through thick jungle. A further liana bridge can be found in Drongouineu, which can be reached by car.

Accommodation
Inexpensive lodgings in Hotel Tia Etienne near the market or - a bit more comfortable - in Hotel des Lianas.

Tai National Park
The Tai National Park is the largest protected **virgin rain forest** in West Africa, an area of 330,000 hectares. The thick vegetation with giant trees up to 60 m high is the home of the chimpanzee, hippo, forest elephant and a variety of birds and insects.

The preserve is not open to visitors, so there is **no possibility of entrance with a vehicle**. Only from the small jungle village of Tai can you get an idea of this extraordinary area.

From Man the route leads over an asphalt road to Guiglo, then further on a track to Tai (bush taxi). Near the village you will find a research station. From Tai, heading south along the border to Liberia, there is no public transport.

Biankouma

Small administrative town 44 km north of Man. Worth seeing is the old, part of the town with its round, straw-covered huts on the slope of a hill. The clay houses are decorated with native paintings in kaolin. The representations give a clue to the inhabitants of the huts: hunting scenes, work in the fields, or initiation ornaments.

The way of life of the inhabitants is still strongly bound to tradition. Biankouma is also famous for its acrobatic Goua dances. The village chief must be contacted before visiting the village! No lodging.

Gouessesso

Along red clay tracks and through hilly jungle the village of Gouessesso is 12 km west of Biankouma. It was here that the Ivory Coast tried to integrate tourism into the countryside for the first time.

A hotel village with round huts fits in well with the surroundings and is in harmony with the original old village.

Blacksmiths, carvers, and weavers don't seem to be bothered by the presence of visitors, the daily life of both villages merge with one another.

The pleasant climate and the spectacular surroundings offer possibilities for excursions and walks. The Yacoubas of this region are famous masked dancers and craftsmen. Nearby is a small liana bridge.

Touba

This region was earlier the home of the Toura, who were famous **magicians**. Today, the Malinké, who came from the north, live here.

A visit to **Zala** in the outlying forested mountain region is well worthwhile. Heading south along a road 15 km from Touba, and turning left along a track you will come to this small village located on a cliff with huts leaning into the mountain slope. The craftsmen of this village create mats with geometrical figures out of raffia. From nearby Mount Zala there is a fantastic panoramic view.

Between Touba and Zala is the tiny village of **Goudofouma**. The original stilt dances take place here where the masked dancers do acrobatic balancing acts on 3 m high stilts.

Accommodation
- Hotel l'Escale, simple lodging with 10 air-conditioned rooms, 707063.
- Hotel Mahou, 22 rooms, swimming pool.

THE NORTHERN REGION

Grass savanna and small bushes, mango trees and bizarre baobabs, round-hutted villages and wide fields characterize the landscape of the north. It is the land of the **Senoufo**, who have never belonged to a kingdom in their past and therefore have been able to keep the customs of their forefathers. As farmers they work the land, plant rice, peanuts, millet, cassava and cotton. The unusual feature of this tribe is seen in their **religious tradition** and in their creative abilities.

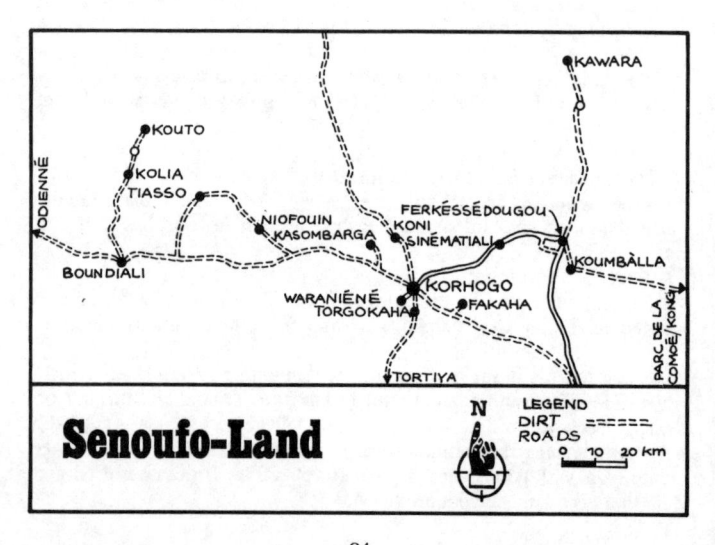

African artwork is not art for its own sake, but has special **ritual significance**. Pottery and carvings, metalworking and traditional architecture have functional purposes, but their designs also have religious and mythological significance. This is especially clear in the items made by the Senoufo, who have, despite many outside influences, kept their own symbolism. The **Senoufo masks** play an important rôle for secret societies, being a means of reaching the good gods and driving away the bad spirits. Only after the dance movements begin are the powers of the masks released.

The imaginative world of the Senoufo is ruled in most part by animal motifs which are clearly seen in the sculptures and statues: crocodiles, monkeys, chameleon and turtles are their symbols, since they are, according to belief, the first four animals created. The sign of this tribe, the ox-pecker (calao) with its spread out wings, is regarded as the symbol of fertility. Even doors of houses and silos as well as drums, spoons, stools and wooden barrels are decorated with these figures.

This animal symbolism is also seen on **linen paintings** which are a speciality of the Senoufo and their relatives in Mali to the north and Burkina Faso. These paintings were previously used for the costumes of the initiated, and for hunters and dancers, today they are mostly made for tourists. But they are still done according to the old tradition: the dyes are made from leaves, bark and iron-bearing clay and are placed onto the unbleached linen with the blade of a knife. You can find this work being done in the villages in the area around Korhogo.

Weaving is done exclusively by men, the spinning and spooling of the threads, on the other hand, is done by the women. Under shady trees in the village square the weavers sit at simple, Sudanese foot-looms and make cotton bands as wide as a hand, which are later sewn together into clothing and blankets. Next to white, indigo blue is used most.

Today cotton is processed in factories in the Ivory Coast making the craftsmen's work easier. The patterns and weaving techniques are still from old traditions. In the region around Korhogo there are several thousand weavers at work in the villages.

Because of its close association with the earth, metalworking has taken on a special social position within society. Smiths are respected because they produce weapons and important instruments for work in the fields. Metalworking in Africa is still connected with belief in magic. The metalsmith, therefore, lives on the edge of the village and often takes on the rôle of master of ceremonies, gravedigger or fortuneteller. Working with iron is one of the oldest types of craft in the north and continues to be done as it was hundreds of years ago.

The **smiths** from Kouto and Kolia (Korhogo region) collect the iron-bearing minerals from narrow, long, vertical shafts, wash it in the river and the clay-like sand is then processed into iron. Leather bellows are used to kindle their fires. Only on Fridays, the holy day of rest, is work taboo.

The **"lost wax" (yellow casting) technique**, a typical African art form, is used in creating jewellery, figures and relief masks. As early as the 11th century the skill of yellow casting has been known in West Africa pro-ducing very fine bronze. First a model is formed out of wax, covered with a layer of clay and dried. The model is heated and the melted wax flows out. Through a connecting canal the liquid metal is poured into the clay cast. As soon as it is cold, the clay is broken, revealing the bronze model. With this method gold can also be exquisitely moulded, but talented craftsmanship is a prerequisite. In the north this method of yellow casting is used in the area around Korhogo.

Odiénné

Heading north from Man is an asphalt road which goes through the beautiful wooded mountain region along the border with Guinea to Odiénné, 274 km away. Since the **black market** flourishes in this border region there are many police and military controls often resulting in long delays.

The city itself does not offer much for tourists, many modern build-ings have taken over from traditional architecture. Near the large mosque is the grave of the Malinké warrior Vakaba Touré who founded Odiénné and who made it into the capital of his Islamic kingdom. The Malinké are a majority in the north.

Odiénné is located in a wonderful valley, under the 800 m high **Massif du Dienguélé**. The hot dry climate of this region is ideal for fruit (mangos, mandarines, guavas, grapefruit).

Arrival
There are regular flights from Korhogo and Abidjan.

Long distance buses run from Abidjan and bush taxis from Man and Korhogo.

Accommodation
- Campement Hotel, near the post office, simple rooms with air-conditioning or fans, about CFA 2,000-4,000. Across from good *Maquis*.
- Hotel des Frontières, small bungalow hotel, nicely located, 30 air-conditioned rooms with showers, restaurant, swimming pool (often no water). Sometimes electrical blackouts. Appropriate prices, tel. 800405.
- Catholic Mission, not far from the post office, simple and cheap.

Area Around Odiénné
Excursion to Mont Dinguélé: 12 km west by vehicle then a half day's climb by foot (a guide and a good supply of water are recommended for this journey). From the summit there is a spectacular view of the surroundings. About 5 km north of Odiénné near the village of **Logonasso** are located two small lakes formed by the dammed river Baoulé. Here you can fish.

Do not swim, as there is a risk of bilharzia!

In the town of **Samatiguila**, 38 km north of Odiénné, you can see a well-preserved 17th century adobe mosque and in the small attached museum with very beautiful weapons from the time of the hero Samory displayed as well as other historical artifacts. Samatiguila can be reached by bush taxi from Odiénné.

Boundiali
The route between Odiénné and Boundiali is one of the very few main roads not asphalted. Through an exotic, hilly landscape this road curves by small villages until it reaches Boundiali, 136 km east on the western border of Senoufo country. The people, who are agricultural experts, cultivate fruit and vegetables, supporting themselves through the cultivation of cotton.

Apart from the market the town itself has little to offer, but is an ideal point of departure for trips into the interesting outlying region.

The outlying Senoufo villages with their traditional round-hut architecture have remained very much in their original form. If the inhabitants are not working in the fields, they are busy with crafts and metalworking, weaving and potting or celebrating one of their numerous ceremonies. If you have enough time you can stop in one of the villages. It is a custom to greet the chief or the oldest person of the village.

Worthwhile is an excursion to the village of **Kouto** which is 31 km towards the Mali border. Noticeable is the division of the town into an Islamic Dioula district and Senoufo animistic quarter. It is especially clear here how modernization increasingly displaces the old traditional adobe architecture.

The new buildings seem quite incongruous beside the well-preserved 17th century **Banco mosque**, beautifully constructed in typical Sudanese style with surrounding adobe walls. In the village square, under the shadow of mango trees, the Senoufo do their weaving. Accommodation can be found in the Catholic mission in Kouto. On the way back to Boundiali stop at **Kolia** where there is a pottery crafts centre.

Korhogo

An asphalt road connects Boundiali with Korhogo, the capital of the northern district. The trip takes you through savanna and by many Senoufo villages, each with its own 'Holy Forest'. From afar Mount Korhogo can be seen, rising up from the plain, the town at its foot. Despite its size (pop. 45,000) the town is quiet and pleasant and, along with Man in the west, is one of the main tourist attractions in the country.

The market is worth seeing above all, offering as it does a lively gathering point for traders with all sorts of goods and articles, especially woven and dyed material from the north. Crafts are bargained for along the street to Hotel Mount Korhogo. The Senegalese traders, who spread out their masks and sculptures of wood and bronze under the mango trees, are very hard bargain-ers. You can get an idea of prices at 'Centre Artisanal', a government-run art exhibition, where you can also see artists at work. Further art centres are near the large mosque.

Those who are more interested in the expressive Senoufo masks, will find an impressive exhibition in **Gbon Coulibaly Museum**. The Senoufo, who live in the north, are not only extraordinary craftsmen, but have been able to keep their strong traditions alive despite the many influences they have been subjected to over the years.

The different dances, whose ritual backgrounds vary according to the occasion, include dance of the metalworkers, dance to honour the dead, as well as thanks for the harvest or for the celebration of Poro (see *Religion*). In the Soba quarter a festival to the rhythm of the balafons and tom-toms is celebrated usually on Saturday evenings.

From the tower of the large, beautifully decorated mosque is a wonderful view of the city and Mount Korhogo (ask for permission before entering the mosque.)

In contrast to this Islamic construction is a small modern Catholic Cathedral (next to the mission). According to the missionaries it is overflowing on Sundays, a sign of the increasing Christianization of this area ruled by animism and Islam in the past.

Arrival
Several weekly flights between Korhogo and Abidjan, Bouaké, Odiénné. Long-distance buses from Abidjan, bush taxis from Ferkéssédougou, Boundiali, Odiénné and many other smaller places.

Accommodation
- Hotel Le Mont Korhogo, not far from the market and city centre. Most expensive and best hotel in the city with 55 air-conditioned rooms (about CFA 14,000). The hotel has a restaurant, bar, disco, and a nice garden with a swimming pool, tel. 860400.
- Motel Agip, next to the bus station. Well-run small hotel with air-conditioned rooms (about CFA 6,000). The restaurant with a shady terrace is recommended, tel. 860113.
- Motel du Centre La Voute, half way between the mission and the post office antennae, reasonably priced.
- Hotel Non Stop, Quartier 14 (street left of the town hall square), 30 air-conditioned rooms, bar, restaurant. Inexpensive lodging, tel. 860793.
- Mission Catholique, simple, but very clean rooms for about CFA 2,000, showers separate. Next to the Cathedral, the missionaries give out information on possible excursions.
- Hotel Liberté, in Quartier 14 near hospital, 20 min. by foot from the centre. Very clean, rooms with air-conditioning and shower.

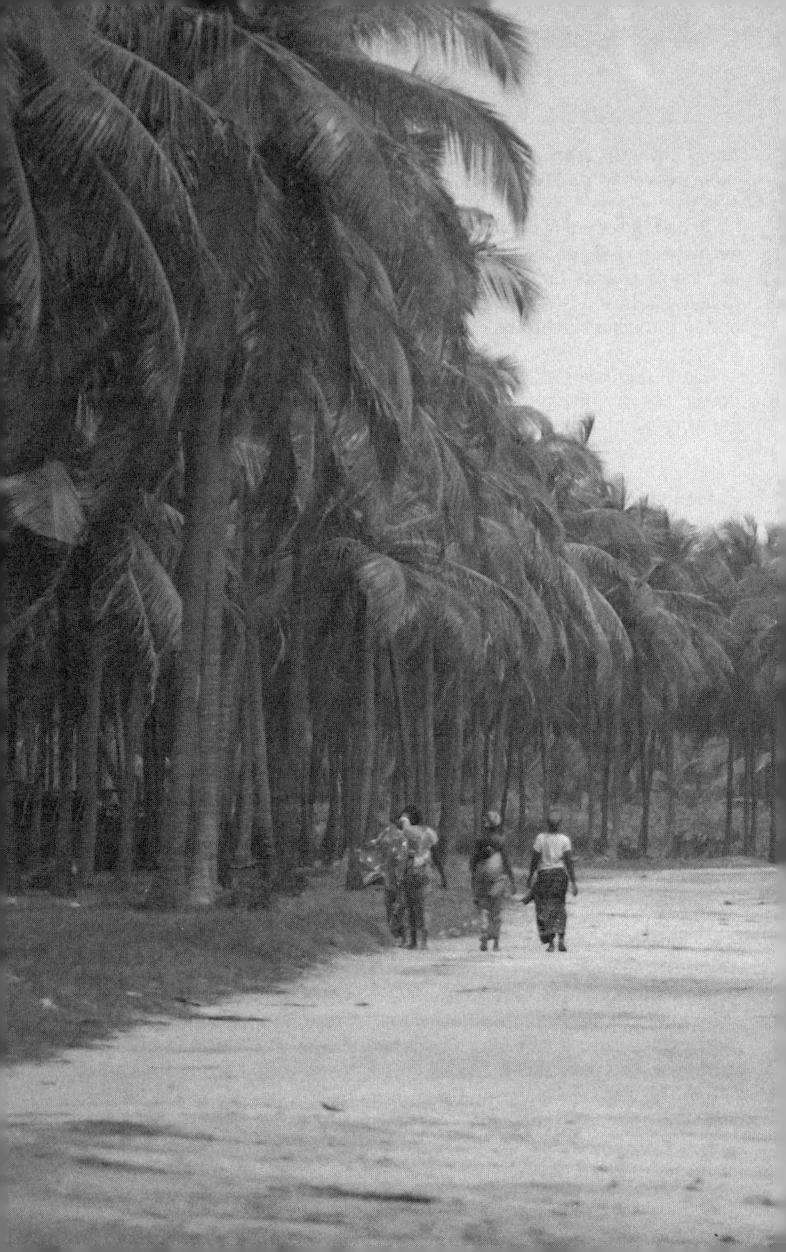

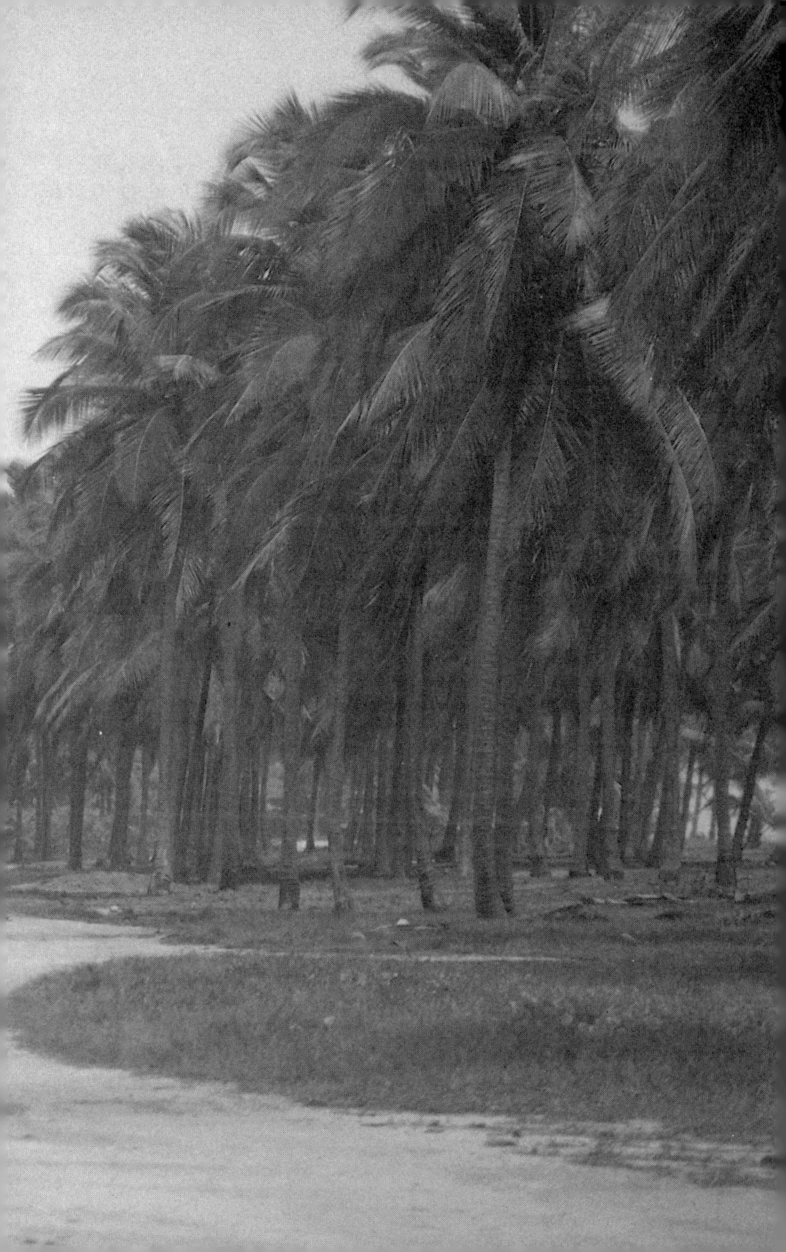

Restaurants
- La Bonne Cuisine, Senegalese cuisine, in the street near the mosque.
- Restaurant la Plantation, Ivory Coast and Senegalese food, good and inexpensive.
- Hotel Agip, excellent French cuisine.

Korhogo has a post office and telegraph office, pharmacy, hospital and numerous banks. Central bus station near the market, another near Hotel Agip.

Area Around Korhogo
Korhogo is the departure point for a variety of interesting excursions into the surroundings, e.g. to Mount Korhogo. The summit can be reached in little more than an hour's walk from the centre of the city, there is a fantastic view. This region is interesting for the many small villages near Korhogo, each specializing in certain crafts made during the dry period, when the fields are not being planted.

If you don't have your own vehicle, you can ask the tourist office in Korhogo where excursions are organized and taxis are rented. The bush taxis, however, are not reliable.

Waraniéné
6 km southwest of Korhogo. A village of weavers. Linen is for sale here.

Koni
13 km north of Korhogo. This is a village of metalworkers. Iron ore is mined near by which is processed in the traditional way in clay ovens and later made into field instruments.

Kasombarga
25 km northwest of Korhogo. Metalwork also takes place here. Worth seeing is the beautiful 17th century mosque.

Torgokaha
7 km south of Korhogo. The inhabitants weave baskets and mats.

Fakaha
35 km south east of Korhogo. The inhabitants of Fakaha certainly create the most famous artwork in the Ivory Coast: linen wall hangings

by the Senoufo. Mythological and religious artifacts as well as animals serve as motifs: the same symbolic designs featured on the Senoufo masks. With the help of a sickle-like knife the artist paints the hand-woven, unbleached linen. The dyes of red, brown, and black come from the bark and leaves of trees.

Niofouin
About 50 km west of Korhogo, well-kept houses of old Senoufo architecture with thick straw roofs.

Tortiya
Via Dikodougou along a 122 km road south. This town of diamond and gold diggers drew numerous adventurers. Marius, an old man from southern France, has dreamed for 20 years now of a lucky strike and tells intriguing stories about the place. He also offers accommodation (room CFA 5,000) and excellent food in his small restaurant.

Ferkéssédougou
Ferké, as the Ivory Coast people of the north have nick-named their town, was first founded in the 19th century and has a very modern face. As one of the major intersections in the country, it has become a lively business and trade centre. Besides the cultivation of rice, cotton, tobacco, corn and millet, Ferké has won economic importance through the large sugar cane plantations and refinery located here. The city itself offers very few attractions.

Surroundings
A visit to the small village of **Kawara** with its 17th century Banco mosque, 98 km to the north, can be recommended. (The mosque in Kouto near Boundialis is, however, prettier.) When driving west from Ferké, after 20 km you will come to the small town of **Sinematiali**, with an interesting crafts centre (potters, metalworkers, carvers). The small Nafara tribe also lives here, famous for its expressive dances (dance of the metalworkers, mask dance, etc.). Those continuing their trip south can climb the 600 m high Mount Niangbo (115 km) which offers an impressive panorama of the plains.

Accommodation
- Le Relais Senoufo, medium priced hotel, 32 air-conditioned rooms in bungalow style, swimming pool, restaurant, centrally located, tel. 880323.

- La Réserve, small, simple hotel with 12 air-conditioned rooms, restaurant, swimming pool. Nice location at the entrance to town on the road to Katiola, tel. 880185.
- Hotel Koffikro, simple and clean, rooms with fans or air-conditioning, located near the Total gas station.
- Hotel La Muraille, rooms with fan. Simple, very inexpensive hotel. In the street across from the C.E.G.

An inexpensive and good meal can be found at Hotel La Réserve or in the *Maquis* 'Les Acacias' near the Mobil petrol station.

Kong

On the way from Ferké to Comoé National Park in the east, is Kong, a historically interesting place: a visit is well worth your time. The town was founded in the 12th century by the Senoufo, coming from the north. Its significance in trade and artwork came first in the 17th century under the Malinké, who made it the capital of their kingdom.

As the great centre of African Islam, the influence of the city reached far beyond the borders of the country. Unfortunately Kong was burned to the ground by the famous Malinké warrior Samory in a military expedition against the French.

Today the mosque, the previously very influential Koran school and a few clay houses with roof terraces are reminders of the prosperous time of the city when caravan leaders, faithful Moslems and tradesmen came here. You will also find, as in Kouto, Sudanese architecture with minarets from which horizontal wooden planks support the outer walls. The population of the city consists mostly of the Islamic Dioula, who, besides trade, are also farmers and artists.

Accommodation

Campement Hotel, simple rooms or further to Comoé Safari Lodge on the northern edge of the National Park.

Comoé National Park

From either Ferkéssédougou or Kong there are roads which lead to Nassian and cross the Comoé river at the small village of Ferké (Poste de Kafolo). From this point it is only a few kilometers to the northern entrance of the Park.

Comoé National Park

With an area of 11,500 km², Comoé National Park is one of the largest protected nature preserves in West Africa. Even though the animals of West Africa cannot be compared with those of East Africa, a visit to this area, declared a National Park in 1968, is well worthwhile.

The savanna landscape is characterized by wide, open grass plains which alternate with brush and forested hilly ranges. The Comoé river flows from north to south, 230 km through the reserve which is named after this river.

Along the banks of the wide river is an arcade of forests where elephants live. Their numbers are rather small and you can seldom see them, since poaching has made them wary. Although hunting is strictly forbidden, the park rangers are unsuccessful in bringing poaching under control because of a lack of funds.

Most of the small waterfalls in the park dry up between December and May, the dry period, the remaining water holes are used by hippos and crocodiles. The park is also home to buffaloes, wart-hogs, various species of monkeys, and a multitude of birds, especially numerous near the water. You will most often see the numerous varieties of antelopes, such as the widespread kob and the graceful oribi. The number of predators is quite small, lions, leopards and hyenas can only be seen if you are very lucky.

The National Park is only opened during the long dry period between December and the middle of May, during the rainy season most of the tracks are impassible and the grass is too high for observing the animals. The best time of day for stalking are the early morning hours and the twilight hours; during the midday heat the animals take cover in the shade. At night you are only allowed to drive with a special permit. You are generally not allowed to leave the marked paths: the speed limit is 40 km/h.

Crossing the park from north to south or vice versa takes about 8-10 hours and is a very strenuous trip. At the park entrance you will receive - when available - a map of the tracks and paths, most of which are well marked. Here you can also ask for a guide. When going by vehicle make sure that you take enough petrol, spare tyres, tools and drinking water; the park is very large and seldom driven through.

Liana Bridge in Lieupleu

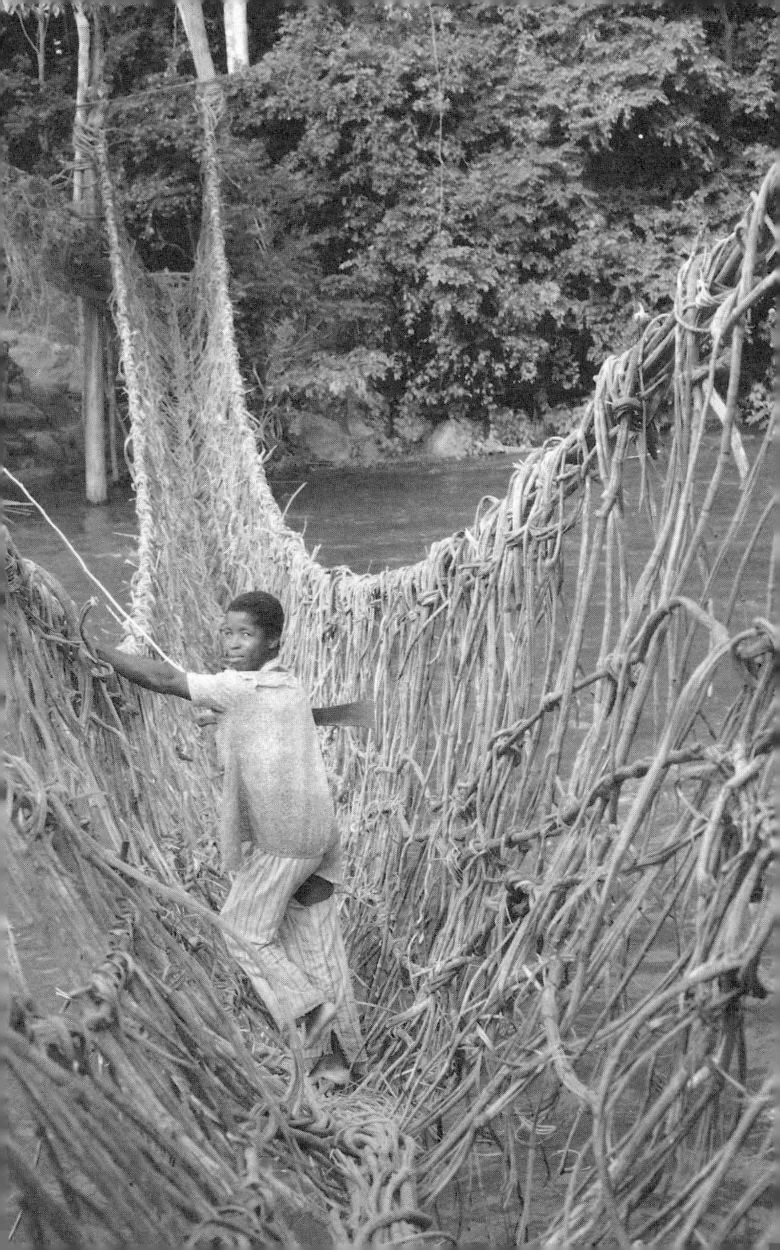

Points of Arrival and Accommodation
At the southern park entrance, Gansé: From Ferkéssédougou 280 km, from Katiola 160 km, from Bondoukou 180 km, all via tracks.

Accommodation in Hotel Comoé, opened from December to May, 25 rooms, restaurant, bar, petrol available. Campement de Kapkin, 16 km from Gansé, very simple round huts for those wanting to be self-sufficient. Inquire about when open.

At the northern park entrance, Ferké: From Ferkéssédougou 121 km (via Kong 185 km), from Bouna 175 km. Accommodation at the Comoé Safari Lodge, opened December to May, well located on bank of the Comoé river, air-conditioned rooms with shower, restaurant, swimming pool. Another park entrance is to the east of Bania, there is no accommodation there.

THE EASTERN REGION

The lushly vegetated area of southeastern Ivory Coast has attained an important economic position through agriculture, unlike the barren northeast, which is sparsely populated. Two important tribes live along the border between Aboisso and Bondoulou: the **Agni** and the **Abron**. They belong to the larger Akam tribe and were forced into exile from Ghana in the 18th century. In the Ivory Coast they founded their own kingdom and have managed to keep their own social structure.

In the far northeast are the Lobi, one of the oldest tribes who have also kept their own way of life. Coming from the upper reaches of the black Volta they were at first semi-nomadic, but with time they settled and today are farmers. Because they are excellent hunters they train their children in the use of the bow and arrow. Especially noticable is the characteristic adobe architecture. The area of the Lobi is connected to the wide expanses of the Comoé National Park, and almost reaches the Burkina Faso border.

Abengourou
An asphalt road runs through a lush forested area with many plantations from Abidjan to Abengourou, 210 km to the northwest. The surrounding area of this city of 40,000 inhabitants is one of the main cultivation areas for coffee and cocoa.

A visit to Abengourou reveals the history and social structure of the **kingdom of the Agni**. Members of this tribe were forced into exile from Ghana and after many hardships settled here to farm the area. Their influential past remains. They observe a hierarchy under the leadership of a **monarch**. Together with his royal household, the King of the Agni resides in the King's Palace in Abengourou, built in 1882, and gives audiences and displays his treasures to guests.

Coming from Ghana, the Gold Coast at that time, gold has always been a symbol of power for the Agni. Therefore, they decorate those being honoured at ceremonies with heavy jewellery. In the Palace Museum you can also see the King's throne 'Bia' which is covered in gold and which is brought out at special processions as a symbol of royal power.

Accommodation
- Hotel Indenie, comfortable hotel with air-conditioned rooms, bar, restaurant, swimming pool, tel. 913159.
- Hotel de la Forêt, simple and clean hotel, air-conditioning, tel. 913729.
- Hotel Asibar, inexpensive lodging near the market.

Surroundings
40 km southeast of Abengourou is the small village of **Zaranou**, the previous capital of the Indenie Kingdom. In the Zaranou museum are exhibitions of art and historical objects: weapons and military uniforms from the time of the colonial governor Binger; old weights for gold, gold miners' hand tools, and beautiful Agni statues, mostly of women in reference to the matrilinear system of the tribe.

When the village chief of Zaranou receives you he will tell you the many legends in which the history and origins of the kingdom are incorporated, and explain the cultural background of inheritance and funeral ceremonies at the death of a king. On some occasions an audience will be enriched by traditional dances.

On the route from Abengourou heading northwest through Agnibilekrou you come to **Takikroum**, at the border with Ghana. At the border everything is strictly controlled and you must expect a long delay. If necessary, accommodation is available on the Ivory Coast side of the border.

Regional Guide

Bondoukou

The city of Bondoukou, 210 km north of Abengourou, was founded in 1466 and during its history was often sought out by conquerers. After smaller tribes fought for the city, the Islamic Dioula created here a prosperous trading post and a very famous **Koran university**. In the years following the city became the capital of the kingdom of the Abron. After the British were defeated near the Gold Coast in Bondoukou in 1888, the city fell into the hands of the French under Binger. At this point the spiritual leader Samory almost entirely destroyed the old settlement. Only the residences of Binger and Samory and the old market building, in which an interesting museum is located today, remain standing.

The great significance of Islam is expressed in no fewer than 18 mosques, whose minarets are visible throughout the city. On the large square in the centre traders and craftsmen meet to sell their jewellery, pottery and dyed cloth.

Arrival
By airplane or bus from Abidjan and Abengourou.

Accommodation
- Hotel du Mont Zanzan, middle priced hotel with air-conditioned rooms, restaurant, and swimming pool, tel. 925414.
- Hotel La Bahai, centrally located with 20 rooms, restaurant, nightclub.

Surroundings
8 km southeast of Bondoukou heading towards Ghana is the small village of Soko, which is entwined in legends. When the warrior Samory threatened this area in the 19th century, the **witch doctor** from Soko wanted to protect the people of the village by changing all the men into monkeys. Unfortunately, the great doctor died before he was able to turn them back into people. Since then the monkeys of Soko have become holy animals which may neither be killed nor eaten. The animals often overrun the market, take delicacies unmolested, and just as quickly disappear into the forest.

Another similar saga surrounds the **Sapia** river, about 18 km west of Bondoukou. The fish living in these waters are holy and are fed daily. They say that when a fish dies, someone from the village will follow!

Dioula Trader at the Market

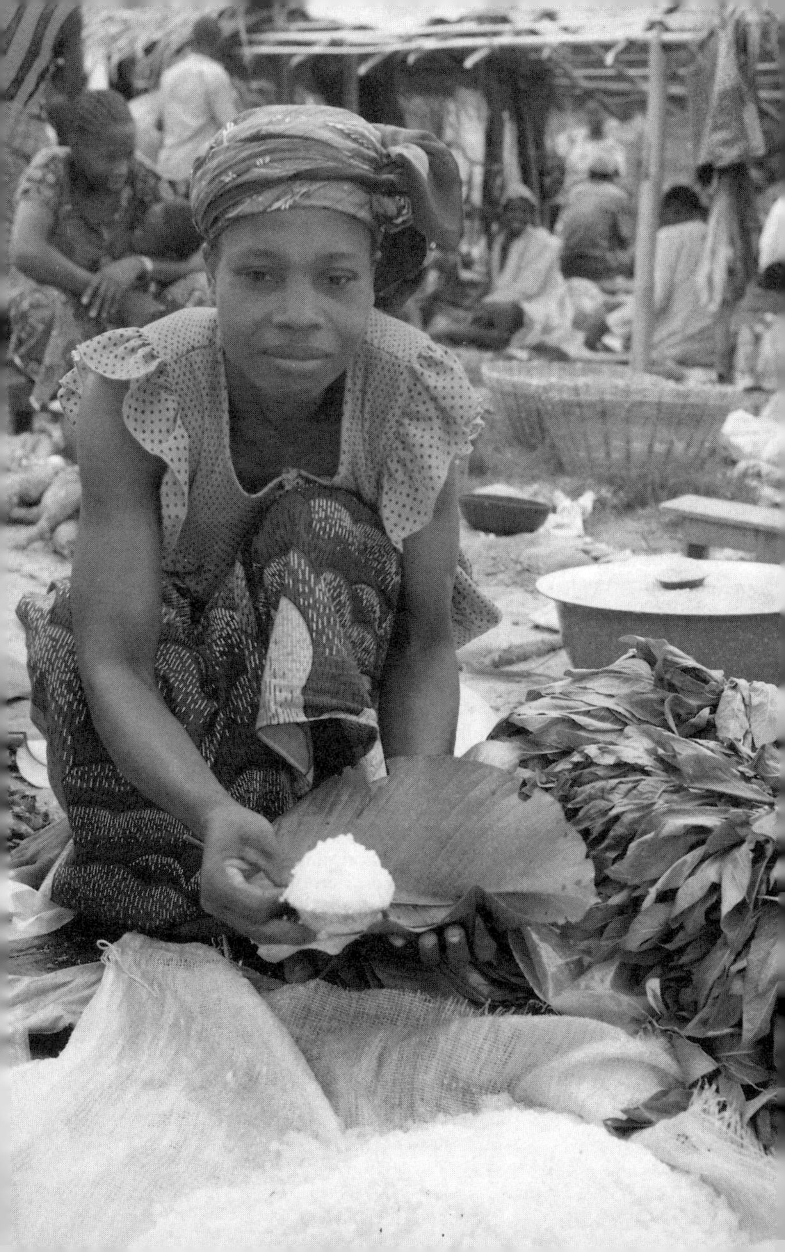

In **Erebo**, 42 km southwest of Bondoukou, resides the **King of the Abron**. This place deserves a visit especially in December when the yearly yam festival is celebrated. During the magnificent procession the king sits in solitary splendour on his throne under a red canopy in his richly decorated toga. Behind him are colourfully dressed laymen and dignitaries. The characteristic gold cult of this once very rich tribe can be seen in the many ornaments.

Bouna

On a track which is passable throughout the year you reach Bouna which is 183 km north of Bondoukou. The **Lobi**, one of the most interesting tribes on the Ivory Coast, live in this region. Most impressive is their unique adobe architecture, called *Soukala*.

These buildings are grouped centrally around an inner courtyard and can be compared with a protected castle, since they are connected by an adobe wall to a farmstead. The construction material consists of a mixture of clay, straw and cow manure and protects against the rain and at the same time is comfortably cool. The *Soukalas* offer space for the entire extended family, which usually consists of many members. A community kitchen and grain silos are in the courtyard.

The prettiest *Soukalas* can be found north of Bouna in the village of **Puon**, which can only be reached during the dry season. In the village of Biénou on the border with Burkina Faso there are other characteristic examples. The Lobi are a very proud, suspicious and shy people. Some women still wear the traditional small, round plate on their upper lip.

The Dioro ceremony, the initiation ceremony which takes place every 9 years, is amongst the most important festivals of the Lobi. Like the Senoufo in the north, boys and girls go through a preparation stage before they are accepted into the adult community.

Accommodation

Campement Hotel, simple rooms, some air-conditioned. Restaurant is on the left side of the road when coming from Bondoukou. The owner organizes excursions into the Lobi villages.

Appendix

Some expressions in Dioula

Good morning, Hello	Ani sogoma (ini sogoma)
Good evening	Ani woula (ini woula)
Good night	ani sou (ini sou)
Thank you	Anitié (initié)

The prefix ani is always used when speaking to several people, ini is used when speaking with one person.

Yes	Onho
No	Oon
Please	Sabari
How much is it?	Djoli-lo?
I would like	N'bafé...
How are you?	Kakene?
I'm fine	Toro si te yen

Index of Place Names

Abengourou	98
Abidjan	11, 47
Aboisso	65
Adjamé	36, 52, 58
Assinie	63
Azagny National Park	68
Azuretti	62
Banco National Park	59
Bandama dam	70
Bandama river	66, 73
Biankouma	83
Bingerville	8, 64
Bondoukou	100
Bouaflé	40, 76
Bouaké	74, 75
Boubélé	72
Bouna	102
Boundiali	87
Bregbo	64
Cascades	81
Cocody	48
Comoé National Park	20, 94
Daloa	76
Danané	82
Ebrie lagoon	64, 66
Erebo	102
Facobly	82
Fakaha	92
Ferkéssédougou	93
Glonguin	82
Gouessesso	83
Grand Bassam	8, 59
Grand Béréby	71
Grand Lahou	38, 67
Ile de Tiegba	66
Jacqueville	65
Kasombarga	92
Katiola	41
Kawara	93
Kolia	86
Kong	94
Koni	92
Korhogo	88
Kouto	86, 88
Labléko	70
Lateko	70
Logonasso	87
Man	10, 78, 80, 81
Maraoué National Park	76
Marcory	50
Massif du Dienguélé	86
Ménéké	73
Mount Tonkoui	81
Niezeko	70
Niofouin	93
Odiénné	86, 87
Plage de Vridi	59
Plateau	48
Poliplage	70
Puon	102
Samatiguila	87
San Pedro	70
Sapia river	100

Sassandra	68
Senoufo	41, 84
Sinematiali	93
Soko	100
Tabou	72
Tai National Park	17, 82
Takikroum	99
Tieni-Siably	81
Torgokaha	92
Tortiya	93
Touba	83
Treichville	48, 52
Waraniéné	92
Yamoussoukro	73
Zaranou	99

Notes

Notes

SENEGAL

Christa Mang

AFRICA HANDBOOK

This travel guide gives helpful information for a different kind of holiday. Stay in rural villages amongst the people; experience the traditional festivals, tea ceremonies, unforgettable jungle taxi trips, the busy markets of Dakar and the Niokolo-Koba National Park. Travel routes and important sights are described as well as essential travel tips.

Bradt Publications
41 Nortoft Rd,
Chalfont St Peter,
Bucks
SL9 0LA
UK.

Hunter Publishing, Inc.
300 Raritan Center Parkway
NJ 08818
USA

ISBN 0 946983 54 2

ISBN 1 55650 308 3

AFRICA HANDBOOK

Christa Mang introduces a country unspoiled by tourism. Unique is the word that comes to mind when characterizing Zaire's natural wonders. Who wouldn't get a shiver down their spine when faced by an awe-inspiring yet gentle gorilla in the wild?

Bradt Publications
41 Nortoft Rd,
Chalfont St Peter,
Bucks
SL9 0LA
UK.

Hunter Publishing, Inc.
300 Raritan Center Parkway
NJ 08818
USA

ISBN 0 946983 51 8

ISBN 1 55650 273 7

AFRICA HANDBOOK

MALAWI

A. Hülsbömer
P. Belker

AFRICA HANDBOOK

In Malawi, the 'warm heart of Africa', you will find a wealth of new experiences. The loneliness of the wooded northern highlands, the challenge of climbing in the southern Mulanje mountains, the wonders of diving in the clear waters of Lake Malawi in the only freshwater national park in the world, and the excitement of trout fishing in Nyika Park. Follow the footsteps of David Livingstone and relive the first days of the mission set up in his memory.

You will be left with a memory of a sincere and joyful people, always ready to help the traveller.

Bradt Publications
41 Nortoft Rd,
Chalfont St Peter,
Bucks
SL9 0LA
UK.

Hunter Publishing, Inc.
300 Raritan Center Parkway
NJ 08818
USA

ISBN 0 946983 52 6

ISBN 1 55650 272 9

AFRICA HANDBOOK

OTHER AFRICA GUIDES FROM BRADT PUBLICATIONS

Backpacker's Africa - West and Central
David Else
192 pages. Maps, drawings and photos.
ISBN 0 946983 19 4   £7.95

Backpacker's Africa - East and Southern
Hilary Bradt
208 pages. Maps and drawings.
ISBN 0 946983 20 8   £7.95

Through Africa - A guide for travellers on wheels
Bob Swain & Paula Snyder
Approx 300 pages. Maps, b&w and colour photos.
ISBN 0 946983 65 8   £13.95

Guide to Namibia & Botswana
Simon Atkins & Chris McIntyre
Approx 272 pages. Maps and colour photos.
ISBN 0 946983 64 X   £9.95

Camping Guide to Kenya
David Else
208 pages. Maps, drawings and photos.
ISBN 0 946983 31 3   £7.95

No Frills Guide to Sudan
David Else
64 pages. Maps & drawings.
ISBN 0 946983 15 1   £4.95

No Frills Guide to Zimbabwe & Botswana
David Else
70 pages. Maps and drawings.
ISBN 0 946983 16 X   £5.95